THE GIFT OF THE GAB

THE
GIFT
OF THE
GAB

HOW ELOQUENCE WORKS

DAVID CRYSTAL

YALE UNIVERSITY PRESS
NEW HAVEN AND LONDON

For information about this and other Yale University Press publications, please contact:
U.S. Office: sales.press@yale.edu   yalebooks.com
Europe Office: sales@yaleup.co.uk   yalebooks.co.uk

Typeset in Adobe Caslon Pro by IDSUK (DataConnection) Ltd
Printed in the United States of America

Library of Congress Cataloging-in-Publication Data

Names: Crystal, David, 1941- author.
Title: The gift of the gab : how eloquence works / David Crystal.
Description: Oxford, U.K, : Yale University Press, [2016]
LCCN 2015048302 | ISBN 9780300214260 (hardback)
LCSH: Elocutionists | Eloquence in literature. | Oral
   communication. | Voice culture. | Storytelling. | BISAC: LANGUAGE
   ARTS & DISCIPLINES / Rhetoric. | LANGUAGE ARTS &
   DISCIPLINES / Public Speaking.
Classification: LCC PN4051.2 . C79 2016 | DDC 808.5—dc23
LC record available at http://lccn.loc.gov/2015048302

A catalogue record for this book is available from the British Library.

10 9 8 7 6 5 4 3 2 1

Contents

ELOQUENCE, n.: The art of orally persuading fools that white is the colour it appears to be. It includes the gift of making any colour appear white.

(Ambrose Bierce, 1911, *The Devil's Dictionary*)

Prologue

As long as I can remember, I have had a love affair with eloquence. Perhaps it stems from my mixed Welsh and Irish background, as from my childhood days I recall listening in wonder to my relatives telling stories in dramatic lilting tones, having long and voluble arguments – 'gabbing away', as they would say – about every topic under the sun, and wondering how it was possible to string so many words together so effectively. Or perhaps it was in school, trying this 'gab' out for myself, in front of the class, and being praised for it. And punished too, for being eloquent when I should have been silent. Eloquence, I soon learned, was a double-edged sword.

Was it a gift, this ability to gab? If so, it seemed to be a gift that everyone possessed. When I moved to Liverpool, at the age of ten, I was highly impressed by the humorous, vivid expression of fast-talking, down-to-earth Scousers, who could use sentences as if they were rapier thrusts, and I soon added its character to my Celtic mix. Eloquence got me out of trouble, as I now know it did Peter Ustinov and Billy Connolly, who both found humorous repartee an effective way of evading unwelcome attention from school bullies – the survival of the linguistically fittest.

In secondary school, I was enthralled by an English teacher who showed us how we could stretch our voices to achieve some remarkable effects, and in school plays came to realize that this wasn't just theory, but it could make audiences do some strange things, such as laugh and cry. I did both on my first ever visit to Stratford-upon-Avon, where I learned – thanks chiefly to the powerful, resonant tones of Paul Robeson as Othello – what amazing heights the human voice is capable of achieving.

And so to university, where eventually, as a new lecturer, I had my first real chance to bring together all those experiences into a speaking style of my own, to convey my delight in discovering my second great love affair – with the subject of linguistics. Then a third, when opportunities arose to do some broadcasting. Then a fourth, when invitations started to come in to talk to clubs, societies, and conferences about this new and up-and-coming subject. It dawned on me that life looked as if it was going to be a succession of public-speaking engagements – and so it proved to be.

Being a linguist, I wanted to work out what I was doing that was right, and what had happened if a speech went wrong – when people became restive, started looking at their watches, didn't laugh at a joke, or gave me polite applause. At one extreme there might be rapt attention, and I could have heard the proverbial pin drop; at the other there might be the mutual muttering of those who found their neighbour's utterances more engaging than mine. Public speakers have to anticipate all eventualities, and learn to cope with them, whether it is heckling from the back of the hall, drunken interventions at a wedding reception, or the resonant chime announcing the powering up of a laptop. Sometimes it isn't their fault that things have not gone according to plan. Sometimes it is. It's essential to recognize the difference, and that means learning as much as possible about the way we speak.

I had been trained as a phonetician at University College London, and my first job there, as part of the great Survey of

English Usage, was to explore how the speaking voice was used in everyday settings. My doctoral research had been on English intonation – a central feature of eloquence – and that had involved analysing how great public speakers achieved their successes. I'll be talking about some of them in this book. And it was while I was doing that research that I came to realize that not everyone could speak equally well. It was something I had vaguely noticed at school and as an undergraduate – that some teachers were not very good at getting their ideas across – but the more I spread my listening net, the more I saw that some people were just not very good at public speaking at all. Asking around, I found many who admitted to being scared of it. I lost count of the number of people who, after a talk, came up to me and said 'I could never do what you do.'

This puzzled me. I had to rethink my belief that everyone could – like Uncle Joe in Wales or Richie and his mates in Liverpool – 'talk the hind leg off a donkey', given the chance to do so. There were many, it seems, who couldn't even begin to get the donkey's attention, and who didn't even want to try. I felt this was a great shame, as there's nothing quite like the thrill of successful eloquence, of knowing that you've said what you wanted to say in the most effective way and caused an audience – whether a group of friends, a family gathering, a class of students, or a group of conference delegates – to be delighted, enthused, persuaded, and moved by the way you've said it. So I've written this book to convey something of that thrill, partly to persuade those who think eloquence is not for them that it isn't as far away as they think, and partly to explain to those who've already made some progress in eloquence exactly what it is they have managed to achieve.

Value-added speech

What does 'eloquence' mean to you? If you hear someone described as speaking 'eloquently', what comes to mind? Here are some scenarios:

Jane's father gave a very eloquent speech at her wedding.
Ask Rachel to talk to your club – she's a really eloquent speaker.
The prime minister made an eloquent defence of his policy in the House today.
Smith is one of the most eloquent lecturers I've ever heard.
The archbishop is an eloquent preacher.
My butcher was very eloquent about the quality of his lamb.
You were extremely . . . eloquent, John, when you banged your thumb with a hammer this morning.

There seem to be certain features in common. When speech is described as 'eloquent', I think of it as being:

- fluent – it flows easily and at a good pace, without hesitations, linguistic errors, repetitions, or uncertainty in the use of vocabulary, grammar, and pronunciation;
- personal – it expresses, or appears to express, the convictions of the speaker, whose personality comes across in the choice of language;
- appropriate – it suits the situation the speaker is in, or at least (thinking of the final example) it's an understandable reaction to it;
- heightened – it displays features of artistry that go beyond the linguistic norms we encounter in everyday informal conversation;
- clear – it uses words that are known to the listeners, and puts them into sentences in a way that is easy to understand;
- memorable – it contains elements that stick in the mind, so that if asked, 'what did X say?' it's possible for a listener to repeat tiny bits of it (or, in such scenarios as thumb-hammering, a polite paraphrase of it);
- reactive – it shows awareness of the interest levels and listening abilities of the audience, and responds or adapts to any feedback.

Each of these, of course, operates with varying degrees of success. We can rate someone as fluent but not so clear, or clear but not so appropriate, and so on. You might consider some of the criteria to be less central than others. But for me, top marks for eloquence would go to anyone rated highly on all seven points.

However, not everything we say efficiently can be described as 'eloquent'. There's something odd about:

James Edwards is an eloquent newsreader.
I answered the phone very eloquently.
My doctor gave me an eloquent diagnosis.

The station tannoy eloquently announced the destinations.
Fred told an eloquent joke.

What's the difference? These last cases lack some or all of the seven criteria just outlined. We don't describe as eloquent our routine communications (such as phone-answering and public announcements), impersonal texts read aloud (as in newsreading), repetitions of what has been said before (as in jokes and scripts), or utterances where we are being given information as an end in itself (as in doctor–patient communication). The speakers may be speaking efficiently, and making their point clearly, but there has to be something extra – something more than the intrinsic content of the message – if we're to describe speech as eloquent. The message has to come from the mind and personality of the speaker, and not just be words put into their mouth by some other person, such as a scriptwriter, unless the text is one that welcomes extra commitment on the part of the speaker, and gains from it (such as an impressive reading of a holy text or literary passage).

This last point is critical. When we describe someone as eloquent we acknowledge that we've perceived the individual contribution they've given to their speech, which is a combination of any or all of the following:

- an appeal to our reason – to persuade us;
- an appeal to our feelings – to move us;
- an appeal to our aesthetic sensibility – to delight us.

It's this last factor that is especially associated with eloquence. We *enjoy* it, either as speakers or as listeners. It is, in its most developed state, an art form. We take delight in the experience of manipulating spoken language well, in much the same way that we respond, in our individual ways, to any beautiful human-created object. Everyday speech has no discernible shape, other than that imposed by the normal rules of a language's pronunciation and grammar. Eloquence gives it a perceivable shape that seems to transcend these rules. It is, as literary critic Denis Donoghue puts it, 'speech in excess of expectation'.[1] Value has been added. Eloquence, in this view, has no purpose other than to be itself. It is a form of language play. And that is why some writers – such as Donoghue – are able to extend the notion to include written language along with spoken. For them, eloquence is supremely illustrated by great written literature. But the point applies equally to the eloquence of stand-up comedians.

My focus in this book is solely on eloquence as manifested in speech, and on the means by which spoken eloquence is made possible. For me, it is not primarily a literary phenomenon. Nor is it something to be found only in a few great speakers on special occasions. It's something that we can encounter anywhere, and it can be produced by anyone. There are innumerable everyday situations where we want to be eloquent or are expected to be eloquent. Some are informal – for example, a domestic dispute, an argument in the pub, an angry quarrel with a neighbour, a tearful conversation with a schoolteacher about your child. Some are formal – marketing presentations, sermons, debates, interviews, lectures, funeral eulogies, political addresses, after-dinner speeches and so on. But in all cases we want to get our message across to our listener(s) in the most personal, effective, and satisfying way.

By focusing on speech I don't exclude the use of writing to help achieve an eloquent outcome. People can be eloquent when reading aloud a personally prepared text in an apparently spontaneous way, so that listeners forget (if they ever knew) that a written text is being used. Speakers can make use of notes, slides, PowerPoint, or some other support in such a way that their flow is unimpeded and even enhanced. They will almost certainly have used written aids as part of their preparation, and may even have memorized some of what they're planning to say. Spontaneous eloquence – when someone speaks completely off the cuff, without any preparation or written accompaniment – is actually somewhat exceptional in public speaking. It's there in the question-and-answer session that can follow a talk. And of course it's the norm in fluent everyday conversation.

People do seem able to recognize eloquence when they hear it. So can we say what it is, exactly, in the speech of the 'eloquenti' that they're responding to? Can we explain how it is that some speakers seem able to anticipate and even control the way their audience is going to react? Can we identify what it is that makes us say that someone has 'the gift of the gab'?

As Barack Obama once said, emphatically: yes we can.

Yes we can

That was Barack Obama's slogan in his presidential election campaign of 2008. It wasn't the first time these three words had been used as a slogan. The Scottish National Party had used them in their 1997 general election campaign. And it was the signature catchphrase for television cartoon personality Bob the Builder. But it was Obama who really milked it, with large crowds chanting it during his campaign, and at least two songs composed on the back of it. People now talk of his victory address as the 'yes we can' speech. I'll be exploring what made it work in later chapters.

Eloquence everywhere

Some people do have a gift for eloquence, undoubtedly, just as others have a gift for playing the piano really well. But there's an important difference between eloquence and musicianship. We already know how to speak. The linguistic equivalent to learning musical scales took place when we were infants, and the natural process of language acquisition meant that, by the time we were five, we were already childishly eloquent. Anyone who has had to listen patiently to a long story by an articulate five-year-old will know what I mean. Here is Suzie, aged just four years and seven months, who has decided to retell the story of 'The Three Little Pigs':

One – one day, they went out to build their houses. One built it of straw, one built it of sticks, and one built it of bricks. And he – the little busy brother knowed that in the woods there lived a big bad wolf, he need nothing else but to catch little pigs. So you know what, one day they went out – and – the wolf went slip slosh slip slosh went his feet on the ground. Then – let me see, er – now I think – he said, let me come in, you house of straw. And he said, no no by the hair of my chinny chin chin, I will not let you come in. Then I'll huff and I'll puff, and I'll puff, and I'll blow your house down. So he huffed, and he puffed, and he puffed, and he puffed, and he blew the little straw house all to pieces . . .

The tale goes on in this way for nearly two minutes. It is full of dramatic tone, copying the way she's heard the story read to her, and using some of its phrases accurately, but the retelling is much more than a memorized copy. It shows awareness of audience ('you know what'), active processing ('let me see'), adaptation of what she's heard ('the little busy brother'), and her own personal style (and grammatical level – 'knowed'). These are all features that are needed for adult eloquence.

Nobody taught Suzie to do this. It was her idea to tell the story, and she'd not told it to anyone before (as far as her parents knew). There are occasional hesitations, but on the whole the words tumble out at quite a rate, reflecting the dynamic of the story. At this point, she had been alive for only 1,671 days. She illustrates perfectly my belief that healthy children are naturally eloquent. And while only some will grow up to become adult virtuoso speakers, all of them – all of us – have the potential to achieve a significant level of eloquence.

Some cultures take this for granted. They assume that everyone is eloquent, or has the potential to be so. In the British Isles, the Irish surely take the lead here, symbolized by the practice of kissing the Blarney Stone at Blarney Castle, near Cork, which promises to confer the gift of the gab on those who manage it. But not far behind come Cockney barrow-boys, Liverpool dockers, Welsh and Scots preachers and storytellers, Caribbean and African performance poets and rappers, and a host of others.

Every country could produce a similar list. In some cultures eloquence is so highly valued that oratory has become an artistic skill expected of everyone. It can take the form of storytelling in gatherings, marking a particular occasion in the year (such as harvest time) or time of day (round a fire at night-time) or a point in someone's life – or death (for wakes can elicit excellent stories of the deceased). It can take the form of ritual competitions, in which speakers seek to outdo each other in politeness, joking, boasting, ingenuity, or insults. They might be nationally or locally organized, or totally unpredictable, as when two teenage street gangs pass by each other and, rather than fight, exchange sophisticated insults – 'verbal duelling'. Such eloquence goes by many different names around the world – 'sounding', 'signifying', 'woofing', 'rapping and capping', 'liming and blagging', 'playing the dozens', 'talking sweet', 'fancy talk' . . .

Countries that value speech artistry also illustrate how eloquence is not something for a gifted few, because everyone participates. Several parts of the world have oral poetry contests, often musically accompanied or sung. For example, the *bertsolari* ('improvised verse singer') poetry contests in the Basque region of northern Spain require contestants to improvise a verse according to strict rules of line length and rhyme. The verses are sung, but without musical accompaniment. The *bertsolari* might be given a free hand, or constrained by having to present a particular topic or to incorporate a particular word or group of rhymes into the verse. Pairs of singers may compete together, in the manner of battle rapping (see Interlude 6, p. 45).

An equivalent challenge in English might be: 'compose a verse of four lines, with seven syllables in the first and third lines and six in the second and fourth; make each couplet rhyme; the topic has to be "riding a bicycle for the first time" and you have to use the word *cake*; start as soon as you're ready, but we're all waiting for you'. The sooner you start, the sooner the judges will be impressed. I suppose the nearest thing to this that I'm familiar with is the 'sonnet slam', where contestants improvise fourteen lines following the traditional rhyme structure. *Bertsolaritza*, by contrast, uses several prescribed verse forms of varying numbers of lines (as few as four, or as many as a dozen). One *bertsolari*, Xabier Auriza, sums it up thus:

Neurriz eta errimaz	Metre and rhyme
kantatzea hitza	the singing word
horra hor zer kirol mota	behold bertsolaritza
den bertsolaritza.	as a form of sport.

A form of sport? At the top level there is a televised national championship, held every four years (most recently in 2013), just like the Olympics. There are provincial and inter-schools championships. But the contests are by no means restricted to such major events. They will be found at all levels and ages, and in diverse social settings, such as local festivals, conferences, taverns, and dinner parties. It is, literally, *performance* poetry: a verse argument evolving in front of an audience in real time, judged in terms of its linguistic dexterity. In a short online video, 'Discover the Basque Country',[2] a *bertsolari* describes the art form:

one thinks and sings at the same time. It all takes place at the same moment. This is what differentiates us from poets, writers or musicians. The creative process and the process of presenting the piece happens at the same time and in front of an audience. Having fun by saying things in the most ingenious way in order to generate a reaction from the public.

This could be a definition of eloquence as a whole.

Times are a-changing

Bertsolari used to be exclusively male, but in the 2009 national championships, a woman, Maialen Lujanbio, took the coveted *txapela* (the winner's beret) for the first time. *Bertsolaritza* also used to be the province of older speakers, but the subject is now taught in schools. And the traditional melodies are being supplemented by modern tunes, to produce a new kind of fusion. In 2015 nine musicians and *bertsolaris* from Gipuzkoa travelled to the USA to perform their 'Bertshow'. The tunes included The Beatles' 'Let it Be' and Bob Dylan's 'Blowing in the Wind'.

Knowing how

Examples such as Suzie's retelling and the creations of young *bertsolaris* are typical of what seems to be a natural inclination for eloquence found in children around the world. If this is so, I wonder why so many people appear to have lost the desire or the ability or confidence to speak eloquently. We often hear remarks like this:

> I don't like speaking in public.
> I really wish I'd said that at the time.
> I can't imagine ever giving an after-dinner speech.
> There's just one talker in our family, and it isn't me.
> When it's my turn to say something, I just clam up.
> I've been asked to give a vote of thanks and I'm scared stiff.
> I'd love to be able to speak like Jenny, but I don't know how.

How did this happen? When did the natural eloquence of childhood desert them? Was it squashed in primary school? Was it a result of an adolescent shyness? Did they have an embarrassing or demeaning experience of public speaking that put them off, perhaps when taking part in a debate? Or was it just a lack of opportunity? There's a long-standing policy in schools of telling children to be quiet, and curriculums traditionally provide few chances for public oral fluency. And I wonder just how many jobs there are that require employees to demonstrate high levels of eloquence (chat-show host, sports commentator, auctioneer, salesperson, preacher, politician . . .). So maybe childish eloquence fades away for lack of use, leaving a latent eloquence, awaiting reactivation.

Whatever the reason for its decline in individuals, there are certainly ways of improving personal eloquence. I've sat in on sessions run by speech trainers and voice coaches, and have worked with groups as diverse as ferry announcers and advertising marketeers, and as long as the motivation is there I've seen people achieve levels of speaking competence that far surpassed their expectations. This is because eloquence relies on a very limited number of techniques which it's possible to teach and learn or (if they've been forgotten) relearn. Knowing what they are is the first step towards becoming more eloquent ourselves, and that is chiefly what this book is about. I suppose achieving a high level of eloquence will ultimately depend as much on personality as on ability; but the more we know about the way language works in the eloquence of others, and the more we can learn about oral stagecraft, the more we can develop a level of confidence that will stand us in good stead when we have the opportunity or obligation to speak in public ourselves.

I'm talking now, of course, about the more formal and demanding settings in which eloquence is valued. I'm not suggesting that the butcher or thumb-banged John from Chapter 1 need to work at their speech in order to convey their feelings. Those situations are an ironic or jocular use of the term 'eloquent'. Real eloquence relates to speech that is of some length and has content involving a degree of sophistication and complexity. And in these situations we have to manage three prerequisites if we want to be described as eloquent.

- We need to have something to say and know that we want to say it to a particular audience in a particular setting.
- We need to understand the needs and expectations of our listeners, so that what we say comes across in a way that gives them satisfaction or a motivation to respond – even if that response is total disagreement. There's nothing in the notion of eloquence that requires listeners to agree with what the speaker has said; but if speech is to be rated as eloquent, it must make an out-of-the-ordinary impact on those who hear it.
- We need to know the ways in which our language (or, in bilingual contexts, languages) allows us to say things in this extra-ordinary way – the powerful possibilities of expression hiding within the pronunciation, grammar, vocabulary, and patterns of discourse that make up the structure of speech.

While the first two points are obviously critical, it's the third that presents the biggest problem when we're asked to 'say something' at a dinner, wedding, or other special event. Most people do have at least a vague idea of what they want to say, or what their audience wants to hear, and they have access to sources that will give them useful ideas. There's no shortage of websites that will tell you the sort of thing you can say at a wedding, for instance. What the sites tend not to tell you is how to put these ideas across personally, convincingly, and effectively – in a word, eloquently.

It's the delivery, in the end, that counts. No amount of preparation or content quality will make up for a bad delivery. The Roman philosopher and orator, Marcus Tullius Cicero, commented that 'Many poor speakers have often reaped the rewards of eloquence because of a dignified delivery, and many eloquent men have been considered poor speakers because of an awkward delivery.' And he recalls the great Greek orator Demosthenes who, when asked to name the three most important elements of rhetoric, replied: 'Delivery, delivery, delivery.'[3] The point was reiterated by Marcus Fabius Quintilianus (first century AD), whose twelve-book *Institutio Oratoria* ('Institutes of Oratory') greatly influenced European thinking about eloquence. Delivery, he says,

> has a wonderful power and efficacy in oratory, for it is not so important what sort of thoughts we conceive within ourselves as it is in what manner we express them, since those whom we address are moved only as they hear ... All attempts at exciting the feelings must prove ineffectual unless they are enlivened by the voice of the speaker, by his look, and by the action of almost his whole body. For when we have displayed energy in all these respects, we may think ourselves happy if the judge catches a single spark of our fire, and we surely cannot hope to move him if we are languid and supine, or expect that he will not slumber if we yawn.[4]

Quintilian aside, an analysis of delivery is the weak point in early accounts of oratory. This probably goes back to the grudging treatment of it given by the Greek philosopher Aristotle (fourth century BC), who in his book on rhetoric – the art of persuasion – comments that delivery 'is not regarded as an elevated subject of inquiry'. 'Nonetheless,' he goes on, 'because the business of rhetoric is concerned with appearances, we must pay attention to it, unworthy though it is, because we cannot do without it.' And he notes that those who do bear delivery in mind are usually the ones who win the prizes in dramatic contests.[5]

For the classical writers, and indeed for many modern writers too, the other elements of rhetoric were more important. To make a good persuasive speech you had to attend to five canons. Here they are, with their Latin names first:

- *inventio*, or invention: you select what you want to say;
- *dispositio*, or arrangement: you decide on the order in which to say it;
- *elocutio*, or style: you choose a way in which to say it;
- *memoria*, or memory: you remember all you want to say;
- *pronunciatio*, or delivery: and then you say it.

Most exposition went into the first three, and this emphasis continues in modern books on the subject. Sam Leith's excellent introduction to rhetoric 'from Aristotle to Obama' devotes twenty-eight pages to invention, twenty-three to arrangement, sixteen to style, fourteen to memory – and eleven to delivery. His primary interest is in the rhetoric of political speech-making, where inevitably there's a great deal to be said about the intentions of the speakers and the content of their speeches.[6]

My approach is the other way round, because it deals with a broader subject than rhetoric. Persuasion is only one of the functions of language, and so only one of the functions of eloquence. Denis Donoghue draws a neat contrast between the two: 'Eloquence means saying the right, beautiful, possible thing, regardless of consequences. Rhetoric means saying the persuasive thing at the right time to the right person or people.'[7] So, we need eloquence in order to persuade, but we don't need to be persuading someone in order to be eloquent. With rhetoric, the focus is always on the intention, whatever that may be. *Why* are you speaking so persuasively? Is it to inform me, make me remember you, make me remember your ideas, attract me, seduce me, sell something to me, con me? Eloquence operates regardless of the intention behind it. Eloquence is optimal delivery, whatever the circumstances. How do people achieve that optimal delivery?

There's a *how* question lurking underneath each of those five canons of rhetoric: how do we select, decide, choose, remember, say? How do we bring all these elements together in order to be judged as eloquent? Aristotle thought delivery was just a matter of using pitch, loudness, and rhythm effectively. As we'll see, there are several other *how* perspectives to take into account; and the most fundamental one, to my mind, is: 'How long have I got to speak?'

Going on and on, not

It's often said that the most memorable speeches are the short ones. A classic instance is the speech by President Abraham Lincoln during the dedication of the soldiers' cemetery in Gettysburg, Pennsylvania, on 19 November 1863. The one that begins: 'Four score and seven years ago our fathers brought forth on this continent a new nation, conceived in liberty, and dedicated to the proposition that all men are created equal.' The whole 272-word speech lasted just over two minutes.

What is less remembered today is that this was the second speech on that occasion. It had been preceded by a speech from Senator Edward Everett, an accomplished orator, that lasted for two hours – a not unusual length for such ceremonies (and indeed Lincoln himself had given speeches of such length in the past). By all accounts, Everett's speech was historically profound, hugely emotive, and very well-received. His elegant craftsmanship can be sensed from his opening words:

> Standing beneath this serene sky, overlooking these broad fields now reposing from the labours of the waning year, the mighty Alleghenies dimly towering before us, the graves of our brethren beneath our feet, it is with hesitation that I raise my poor voice to break the eloquent silence of God and Nature.

But it was totally eclipsed by what followed when Lincoln rose to speak.

Everett recognized the coup. In a note to Lincoln the following day, he wrote: 'I should be glad, if I could flatter myself that I came as near to the central idea of the occasion in two hours, as you did in two minutes.' And he praised Lincoln's 'eloquent simplicity'. Lincoln responded, acknowledging the value of Everett's own speech: 'the whole discourse was eminently satisfactory, and will be of great value, [and] there were passages in it which transcended my expectation'.[8] But, 150 years on, it is the short speech that remains with us.

How long have I got?

It's the first thing we need to know. It takes time to show eloquence, and we have to know exactly how much time we've got before we can decide what to say and how to say it.

Usually we're given plenty of notice. We're asked to 'say a few words' well in advance of an occasion. There are arrangements to be made, after all, and organizers need to have everything in place. So we know the sort of thing we're letting ourselves in for if we agree to be an after-dinner speaker, talk to a lunch gathering, or make a speech at a wedding – or, at a more formal level, if we have to give a lecture, a political speech, or a sermon. But in all cases we need to know how long we've got, or at least what the expectations are. Do we have to allow time for questions? At all costs we need to avoid the suppressed boredom of faces which signal that we are going on for too long. No amount of eloquence can get round that. Anyone who tells an eloquent speaker 'I could have listened to you for hours' is living in a make-believe world. They couldn't.

In some situations, of course, the time frame is dictated by an explicit timetable. In schools and universities, a class starting at, say, 11.10 must finish by 12, otherwise there will be chaos, with one group of students clashing with the next. Conference organizers fear the speakers who overrun and throw out all the carefully planned hotel arrangements for coffee (scheduled, say, for 10.45–11.15) and lunch (between 12.45 and 1.45). 'Never overrun' is the first commandment of public speaking. And if someone holds up a card saying 'FIVE MINUTES LEFT', speakers need to respect it.

We need to keep to time because no amount of eloquence can override audience discomfort. And the sad fact is that discomfort negates everything. People remember the discomfort, not the content. I was outside a lecture hall at a conference once where the speaker overran by a good ten minutes, well into the coffee break. In the coffee queue, someone who hadn't been in the hall asked someone who had how the talk had gone. 'He didn't know how to stop,' grumbled the attendee. The questioner persisted, wanting to know about the content. 'But what was he saying?' The attendee muttered something I couldn't hear, clearly not wanting to talk about it.

One of the biggest dangers – and this applied here, I later discovered – was total dependence on a PowerPoint presentation. The speaker had carefully planned what to say, but seriously underestimated the time it would take to say it. Putting too much information on a screen is a common fault. So when his time was up, he still had several slides to go, and there was no way he could get to the last one, which contained his main conclusions, without flipping through the others, thereby acknowledging he'd got things wrong and making the audience feel even more dissatisfied as they now knew they'd been shortchanged. So he slogged on to the bitter end, inevitably rushing, thereby making his content even more difficult to take in. It was a lose–lose situation.

There's a real problem for speakers if the event fails to start on time. I don't mean a minute or so's delay. I mean serious lateness. I'm often asked to open a conference with a talk at, say,

9.15 a.m., after a fifteen-minute opening ceremony scheduled to begin at 9.00. The coffee break is to be at 10.15, so I know I have a comfortable hour. But 9.05 passes and nothing has happened. Then 9.10. Only half the expected audience has arrived. I ask the organizer when things will start. There is an apologetic explanation: 'We never start on time in this country. It's terrible, but . . .' or 'The traffic is awful at this time of day . . .'

By 9.15, enough of the audience has arrived to make a start. I sit in the front row waiting to be called on stage. The organizer welcomes everyone. And then the welcome extends to a panel of half a dozen local dignitaries, each of whom is going to 'say a few words'. There seems to be only one working principle on such occasions: however long the previous speaker has been, the next must speak longer. I've sometimes not been able to begin until 9.45. And I must stop at 10.15 – or must I? That's the critical question that has to be asked before you begin. How flexible is the timetable? Usually the organizers, knowing the score, have built in some flexibility – but they haven't thought to tell you what it is. Ask. Can I really take my full hour, or must I trim the talk?

In most everyday speaking situations, of course, there's no official timetable, simply an expectation, formed over the years by experience, that the speaker will talk for about N minutes. So it's the first question I always ask when I receive an invitation to give a lunchtime talk, or an after-dinner speech, or a bookshop talk, or whatever. What is N? 'How long have I got?' Organizers usually have an answer. They know, from bitter experience, how much their audience can take before they start to fidget and look at their watches. Distrust any organizer who replies with 'Oh, as long as you like'.

Things tend to go wrong when the organizers of an event have no experience because this is the first time they've had to do it. Wedding receptions are a case in point. For most families, it's a one-off, with those giving the speeches often doing so for the first time. The combination of emotion and alcohol can lead to long and erratic speeches that leave guests auditorily exhausted – though the effect is usually partly compensated for by increased levels of receptivity among the guests, fostered by the same combination. Wedding etiquette guides usually suggest a speech of no more than five minutes. But inexperienced speakers have no sense of the passing of time. I was at a wedding once where the best man had been advised he should speak for five minutes and he'd agreed. He went on, with great sincerity, but to an increasingly fidgeting audience, for twenty. Some tables, furthest from the speaker, switched off completely and started to talk among themselves. When he sat down, I heard him ask the groom: 'Was that five minutes?'

There have been periods in history when the expectation was that a speech (or a sermon) should be long, otherwise it could not be any good. Eloquence was identified with length. The seventeenth-century poet and cleric John Donne regularly gave sermons that lasted two hours or more. Today, in an online world, where brevity is the soul of Twitter, intuitions and expectations about the nature of eloquence are changing. Older people, for whom the book is central and the screen is marginal, still have a predilection for the longer speech, and recall the classic speeches of the past – such as those by Churchill or Kennedy – with admiration, and even affection. Younger people, for whom the screen is central and books are marginal, and where communicative life is largely carried on in texts and tweets – the 'short messaging services' – tend to think in a different way.

But they still need to be eloquent. Eloquence is not constrained by length, but exploits it. So it is perfectly possible to be eloquent in the spoken equivalent of 140 characters, which is longer than you might think – between twenty and thirty words in English. And all public figures know the importance of the 'sound bite' – a short and punchy extract from a longer discourse which is used to summarize or promote the speaker's message. If we think of eloquence as being a truly effective use of spoken language, then we can do a lot with twenty or thirty words. Or fewer. Can we be eloquent even in three words? Yes we can.

I'll talk later about how this sort of thing works. Clearly a short sentence has to be seen in the context of a longer discourse to make sense. But even that longer discourse does not have to be very long to be effective. The popular online TED (Technology, Entertainment, Design) talks are up to eighteen minutes, and no more – 'the length of a coffee break', as TED curator Chris Anderson once said. Here's the context for his remark:

> It is long enough to be serious and short enough to hold people's attention. It turns out that this length also works incredibly well online. It's the length of a coffee break. So, you watch a great talk, and forward the link to two or three people. It can go viral, very easily. The 18-minute length also works much like the way Twitter forces people to be disciplined in what they write. By forcing speakers who are used to going on for 45 minutes to bring it down to 18, you get them to really think about what they want to say. What is the key point they want to communicate? It has a clarifying effect. It brings discipline.[9]

The point goes well beyond TED talks. Anyone can benefit from the discipline of 'thinking in halves': work out what you want to say, in the time you've been allotted, then think how you would say it if you had only half the time.

Knowing how long you've got is the first thing you need to know before you plan what you're going to say. The second thing is to know where you will be saying it.

When you're the boss

President Gaddafi of Libya in the middle of a ninety-six minute speech to the UN General Assembly, 23 September 2009

We inevitably associate eloquence with great public speakers. Not all would satisfy the TED organizers. Martin Luther King would, for his great 'I have a dream' speech came in at seventeen minutes. But Winston Churchill wouldn't: his 'This was their finest hour' speech on 18 June 1940 was thirty-six minutes. Both were brilliant. There is no minimal measure of length that determines the effectiveness of eloquence.

Nor is there a maximal measure. It is of course possible to speak in public for an hour, or hours, or even days. The Guinness Book of Records reports that the longest speech before the UN General Assembly was given by Fidel Castro in 1960, and lasted four hours and twenty-nine minutes. This was short by his standards: at the 1986 Communist Party Congress in Cuba, his speech lasted seven hours and ten minutes. And that, in turn, was short by the standards of Mustafa Kemal Atatürk, the founder of modern Turkey, who spoke in 1927 for thirty-six hours and thirty-one minutes over six days.

You can't get away with that sort of thing unless you're the boss. The picture says it all.

5

Where will I be?

Good speakers never seem to have a problem with the venue. They seem able to adapt themselves to any setting. They make the venue work for them. But it takes a lot of experience to reach that stage. If you're new to public speaking, regardless of whether the event is large or small, taking time to learn about the venue in advance is time well spent. There are so many things that can put you off your stride if you're not ready for them. A noisy air-conditioning system. Outside traffic hubbub. To be eloquent, you need to be in control, and to achieve this you need to know about the setting in order to make your delivery suit the occasion.

None of this requires specialist thinking. Eloquence does have some intricate features, as we'll see later, but being in control of your setting isn't one of them. The issues are pretty basic. How large is the venue, first of all? What shape is the room? And the associated question: how many will be in the audience, and will I be able to see them all easily? Which leads in turn to a further question: will they all be able to hear me? There's not much point in trying to be eloquent if they can't.

So, does the venue need a microphone and, if it does, what kind? To answer that question you have to know yourself as a speaker. Are you the kind of speaker who needs notes or a script? Then you'll be happy with a fixed microphone at a lectern, but make sure it's the right height for you. Are you someone who doesn't use your hands much when you talk? Then you'll be happy with a handheld mike. Are you someone who likes to walk up and down a lot and to reinforce your speaking with your hands? Then you won't be happy unless you have a headset or a clip-on mike, sometimes called a lapel mike (but not so appropriate a term if your clothes happen not to have any lapels).

Does the venue have all these options? If not, it may seriously alter your speaking style and the effectiveness of your presentation. I once turned up to talk at a literary festival being held in a school hall, without having checked in advance. The hall could seat about 500, and the ceiling was very high, so a normal speaking voice would be lost in the space. A conversation at one end of the hall couldn't be heard at the other. The room needed a mike. The school had one, of course – a handheld.

It was a talk where I was giving a lot of Shakespeare examples, and I had them all printed out as a kind of script, on separate pages, one on each page. I didn't know them by heart. Some were whole-body examples too, where the effect was going to be reinforced by head and arm movements, and even, at one point, by a posture change (one character had to kneel before another). The effects work really well in a small, intimate setting which doesn't need amplification; but in a large hall they need a hands-free microphone. 'Have you got a lapel mike?' I asked. They hadn't.

I didn't want to make myself hoarse trying to reach the back of that large hall for a whole hour unaided. So I had to use the handheld. That meant holding the pages of a script in my left hand and the microphone in my right. Not a big problem, you might think. Not until you have to turn the page. Try taking the top page of a sheaf and placing it on the bottom using only one hand. It can't be done. The other hand has to help. But that one is holding the microphone. So either you suddenly become inaudible, or you have to stop talking. Neither is going to give you marks for eloquence. And I had to do it several times. I wasn't happy.

Whatever kind of speaker you are, it'll pay you to check out the venue in advance, and, if a microphone is needed, to learn about its properties. Sometimes it's obligatory, as the venue has an auditory loop to help people with hearing aids. One of the biggest misconceptions about public speaking is that the mike will do all the work. Not a bit. It's a tool, and you have to use it well if it's going to do its job. Not all mikes are the same. Some are omnidirectional: they will pick up your voice even if your mouth is not directly in front of them. Some are unidirectional. Move your mouth away from the front and your voice suddenly becomes distant and muffled.

Many venues use unidirectional mikes because they're used to recording groups of people where the voices or instruments have to be kept apart (such as a pop music band) or where they want to keep out unwanted noise (such as audience reactions). If so, you need to know this, as a unidirectional mike will seriously restrict your movement, whether you're standing in front of a lectern or holding a handheld device. Eloquence demands a comfortable naturalness of expression, and this can easily be disturbed if you're having to concentrate on maintaining a fixed distance between your mouth and the microphone. There are so many factors that can make you move away so that your voice level fluctuates. If you're reading your material at a lectern, it varies when you move your head up (to see the audience) then down (to read your text). Or when you keep talking while you reach for a glass of water. Or when you decide to make an expansive gesture with your right hand, forgetting that your unidirectional handheld is in it.

If there's a technician looking after things, you may not have to worry about sound level – the loudness that your audience hears. But in most everyday settings, such a luxury is absent. The organizers set a fixed level in the sound system, and you're on your own. So you need to know how close you have to be to the mike, whatever kind it is. You don't want to blast people out of their seats by holding it too close. Nor do you want them straining to hear you if it's too far away. One of the most common faults is to be given a handheld and then to hold it somewhere down near your stomach so that it becomes useless. You don't want members of your audience shouting at you to 'Use the microphone!' when you think you are.

Even with a clip-on mike you have to be careful, especially if you're engaged in a dialogue with someone else, such as in an interview. Whether you're the interviewer or the interviewee, the issue is the same. If your partner is seated on your left, and your lapel mike has been attached to the right side of your jacket or dress, then you'll be continually turning away from the mike as you interact. And conversely. So make sure the mike is positioned in front of the way your head is going to be facing.

And know how to turn it on, if the technician hasn't already done so. The on/off switch on a handheld mike can be in the most unobvious of places sometimes. As can the corresponding switch in the device to which your clip-on mike is attached. Opening the cover of the device to find the on-switch can prove an unexpected problem, as you may have to press the sides of the device in a mysterious way. It's worth a check. I'm amazed at how often I find the switch has been left on 'mute'.

A sound-check is therefore an essential preliminary. If there's no technician around to help, get someone to go around the room as you speak into the microphone. Not just at the back, but at the sides and front as well. If the sound echoes a bit, that isn't usually a problem, as when the room fills up the presence of lots of people will help eliminate that. And don't restrict yourself to saying just 'One, two, three', like the professional techies do. Think ahead to the parts of your talk where there may be a loudness shift, such as a punchline in a joke, or a piece of dramatic reading, and try out a bit of it.

If you're going to be moving about, test what happens while you're moving. With some sound systems, if you walk too far forward in front of the amplifiers, the room fills with horrendous screeching. Check where you can move without anything electronically horrible happening. And check if you're wearing anything that might rustle or jangle. Conference lanyard badges especially can be a pain, as they can bump up against the microphone and cause scraping noises. So can beards. I once scared an audience by nodding my head seriously and vigorously in response to a question, with my beard repeatedly hitting the very sensitive clip-on mike placed rather too high up on my tie. The rasping made me sound like Darth Vader.

All of this relates to hearing the speaker. Eloquence assumes efficient auditory delivery. But there's a second dimension, neatly summarized in an old Latin aphorism, thought to be a translation of something from Socrates: *Loquere ut te videam*, 'speak that I may see thee'. The philosopher meant: 'by speaking, you reveal what is inside you'. But the words have a literal application in relation to eloquence, because a great deal is lost if the audience can't see the speaker.

So, look around the room. Can everyone see you? It's surprising how often the answer is no. Many rooms have pillars with seats behind. A 'restricted view', they call it in theatres. If the seats are fixed, there's no way the occupant can move the chair into a better position. In which case, if you want your words to reach that person, you have to do the moving, so that at least some of the time every member of the audience gets a sight of you.

My son Ben told me of his experience of being in the company at Shakespeare's Globe in London. This is a recreation of the original Elizabethan theatre that was built in 1599. The stage thrusts out into a courtyard, and people stand and sit on all three sides. The ceiling above the stage is supported by two huge pillars, one towards the front stage-right, the other towards the front stage-left. That means there's nowhere in the theatre where you can see the whole stage. A pillar is always hiding a part of it.

So, if Hamlet is speaking from behind the left-hand pillar, people to his right and left will see him clearly enough, but anyone in front of that pillar won't see him at all. And if he moves to the right of the pillar, now the people in front can see him, but those to the left of the pillar won't be able to. What actors have to do, then, is move a lot, up and down the stage, so that, for any member of the audience, the pillars become a temporary barrier only a small part of the time. It's a new kind of movement technique, and Globe actors generally handle it brilliantly.

There isn't much difference between actors and public speakers. They share many skills – pace, timing, voice projection … and visibility. Aristotle pointed out the parallel. He says: 'When the principles of delivery have been worked out, they will produce the same effect as on the stage.'[10] Anyone wishing to display eloquence can learn from the acting profession, especially when speaking in an intimate space. You need to be able to see every member of your audience – if not all the time, then at least regularly in your presentation – and this may require you to move around a bit. If this isn't possible, make sure your presentation doesn't depend on visual elements, such as gestures, facial expressions, or handheld objects, such as the cover of a book or a tiny picture of the groom as a baby.

And there's one other thing to remember if you're making a speech that's being filmed – either for an online feed, or for a video conference, or simply because (you should be so lucky) the audience couldn't all fit into the main hall, so an overflow room has been created with a video link. Make sure you know how much of you can be seen, and whether you're being filmed at a distance or in close-up, or both. If at a distance, the people may not be able to see any subtle visual features, such as pulling a face or displaying a small object. If close-up, how much of you is in shot? And is the camera able to follow you around if you move, or capture any expansive gestures? A few words with the camera operators beforehand will help avoid any unforeseen problems.

One must, unfortunately, also be prepared for the unexpected. There are some distractions that it simply isn't possible to defeat, no matter how much preparation you've made, or how eloquent you are. I was talking to a group of speech therapists once at a hospital in Chelmsford in Essex. It was on the second floor in a room overlooking the grounds of the Essex County Cricket Club. The team was playing at home. It was a hot day, and the windows were open. So my entire talk was punctuated by roars from the crowd and shouts of 'HOWZAT?' It was hard to compete, so I tried to build the interruptions into my talk. Fortunately most of my audience, it seemed, weren't interested in cricket, but I did notice that three members had carefully positioned their chairs facing the open window. I don't think they learned much about linguistics that day.

But that paled beside the noise at the 2002 Hay Festival when Ben and I were due to give a talk on our new book, *Shakespeare's Words*. Friday 7 June 2002, to be precise, at 1 p.m. The astute organizers were aware that their festival would coincide with the football World Cup in Sapporo, Japan, so they had arranged a live feed into a large tent. That day, at 20.30 p.m. local time, England were playing Argentina. Japan was eight hours ahead of UK time. Work it out.

We were giving our talk in the marquee next door. And forty-four minutes into the match, at 1.14 in Hay, David Beckham scored a penalty. Ben and I had no chance. You could probably hear the roar in the football tent from the top of Mount Snowdon. You certainly couldn't hear us. The

Argentinians fought back, and England responded. It was evidently a very exciting game. Roars came every couple of minutes (though no more goals). Our poor Shakespearephilic audience had a very tough time. Some surreptitiously kept their mobile phones on, to keep an eye on the score. As did we.

Capitulation

Sometimes the setting wins, and you just have to give up.

In the early 1970s, I was teaching a course on English grammar at a summer school, at the south end of Copacabana Beach in Rio de Janeiro, in the fortnight before Carnival. The temperature was in the nineties, so the air-conditioning was full on and very noisy, and because it wasn't working very well the windows were open too.

I was waxing eloquently about the intricacies of the English noun phrase when I noticed that there was some audience twitching going on. The students had heard what it took me a minute or so more to hear above the traffic. A drum beat. A whole samba school of drum beats. In the distance, but coming nearer. Some of the samba bands were out and about, getting in some practice. And here was one of the best, some twenty musicians and dancers, glittering in their costumes, rhythmically approaching my lecture. There was no point in going on.

My audience was Brazilian through and through, and their pulses were genetically programmed to follow a samba beat. They looked at me appealingly. I gave in.

They were at the windows in a flash, all dancing, and I was given a tutorial on which part of Rio the band was from and what the name of the song was. Due deference was shown to my professorial role, and I was placed mid-window. The band reached us, and we gave it a special cheer. Not expecting such a sizeable audience, they stopped and did an impromptu show – and I mean show. The leading female dancer, dressed – if that is the right term – in three feathers, came up to the window, and homed in on the least Brazilian-looking spectator. I had never seen feathers move in that way before. 'What should I do?' I asked the nearest student. 'Gyrate,' he said. All I could think to say was: 'I don't know how to gyrate. I'm from Wales.'

'I show you,' said one of the male students, and I abandoned my window spot to him. Fortunately the band moved on before I was offered the chance to demonstrate my gyratory incompetence, and the class reconvened. I don't think my eloquence recovered from the setback that day.

6

Who am I talking to?
(To whom am I talking?)

Know yourself? Of course. But know your audience too.

Sometimes it's obvious. At a wedding reception, the attendance is circumscribed by the married couple. You won't know everyone in the room personally, but you can be sure they're all relatives or friends. If you're speaking at a Rotary Club lunch, you know you're talking to people with a diverse professional background. But at a literary festival, for example, you never know who's going to be in the audience. The same applies to any open public meeting, such as a political or religious gathering. So it's always wise to assume that there's someone listening who knows a great deal about your subject.

A few years ago I was giving a talk at the Hay Festival about English accents, and describing the mixed London accent often called 'Estuary English', which was receiving some media publicity at the time. To fix it in the minds of my audience, I thought I would refer to some well-known personalities who spoke with it, and mentioned Pauline Quirke and Linda Robson, the two actresses in the BBC television sitcom *Birds of a Feather*.

After the talk there was time for questions. A man in a middle row put his hand up. He was delighted to hear me talk about *Birds of a Feather*, he said, and he went on to say how the actresses had had to modify their originally broader London accent to ensure that they would be readily understood on national television. I didn't know that background, but I was glad to hear it, because it was an excellent example of the kind of social factor that fosters the spread of new accents.

'You seem to know a lot about it,' I said.

'I ought to,' he replied. 'I wrote it.'

It was Laurence Marks, half of the writing partnership of Marks and (Maurice) Gran.

That's the kind of thing that happens at a literary festival. You never know who's going to be there. So you'd better not make careless literary allusions, as it would be just your bad luck to find the author or critic sitting in your audience. Shakespeare is safe enough, though.

This isn't just a literary danger. It applies to any class of people in your audience, wherever you're speaking, as well as to individuals. Are your listeners old or young, male or female, experts or neophytes? Do they have English as a first or foreign language? If you're speaking overseas, what factors in the country's culture are likely to condition your audience's response?

The age of the audience is especially critical. If it's a young audience, such as a group of teenagers, and you, the speaker, are somewhat less young, then you need to bear in mind the vast linguistic and cultural distance between them and you. Don't fall into the trap of trying to 'speak like them'. The adult speaker who lards a presentation with young persons' slang (words like *wicked*, meaning 'excellent', in the days when this was a popular usage) will receive facial reactions ranging from boredom to contempt. Histrionic, highly crafted eloquence doesn't go down so well either. The modern expectation is towards a more conversational style.

The cultural gap can affect the content of a presentation too. A few years ago I wrote an introduction to language aimed chiefly at students in secondary school, called *A Little Book of Language*. One of the chapters was about pseudonyms, so I included as examples the names of famous people who had replaced their original name by a professional name. People like John Wayne, born Marion Robert Morrison. Before the book went to press I had it read by a twelve-year-old. As it was her first paid job she was delighted to do it. 'Read it carefully,' I told her, 'and underline anything you don't understand.' And when she got to the pseudonyms chapter, she underlined John Wayne.

'Don't you know who John Wayne is?' I asked, horrified.

'No,' she replied, surprised at my surprise.

'You don't know *Stagecoach*, *Liberty Valance* . . .?'

'?'

None of the examples from my world matched hers, which I then had to explore before finding examples her age-group would know. In the end we settled on pop star Eminem and actor David Tennant. But if she hadn't been a *Doctor Who* fan, even Tennant's name wouldn't have worked.

So, when talking to schools, or any group of people seriously younger than you are, never assume that they know the personalities or events you cite when discussing a particular topic. Always check with them, without being patronizing, and be ready to explain. Take nothing for granted. As a historian fellow-lecturer told me, in the green room at a literary festival, after a school visit where he'd spent more time than he intended having to explain who was who: 'Not even Churchill.' And, after a glum pause: '. . . Or Hitler.'

Vast cultural distance. The same principle applies if you're talking to an audience much older than you are. They'll certainly know about John Wayne, but perhaps not Eminem. And linguistically they can be distracted from your content if the way you're talking jars with any conservative temperaments. Irritation destroys the impact of eloquence. Irritation about English usage, especially.

You often don't learn about the way a casual usage has irritated someone until during question time, or in the following break. Tiny details can have a disproportionate effect. I have had individuals publicly object to my splitting an infinitive (*to really see...*), pronouncing **con**troversy as con**trov**ersy, using *decimate* to mean 'destroy' rather than 'kill a tenth', and many more of the usages that the objectors had learned from a lifetime of reverence for Fowler or Strunk & White or some other traditional guide to English usage. I mean *really* object. They begin their 'question' with such language as 'I was appalled to hear you say ...' or 'I can't believe that a professor of English would say ...' They are genuinely upset.

These days, most audiences are more accepting of the processes of language change, and may not even notice such things. Younger audiences are probably as knowledgeable about split infinitives as they are about John Wayne. Overseas audiences, too, tend to disregard them, as they are usually unfamiliar with the history of complaints about points of disputed English usage. So, most of the time, I speak in my natural style, split infinitives and all. But when I'm talking to an older group, I tend to adopt a more conservative style of speech, as I want them to attend to what I'm saying and not be distracted by the way I'm saying it. I try to remember to avoid these contentious usages. Avoidance strategies are part of successful eloquence too.

I don't mean consciously avoid. Because there aren't very many such linguistic points, it's possible to develop a conservative style of speech which flows naturally without having to think about every word as you're saying it. And if you're reading a speech, these points can be ironed out beforehand in the writing. That's what radio presenters do. I've seen news scripts where the readers have underlined a danger point in the text, such as *law and order*, where they don't want to introduce an 'intrusive r' in their pronunciation of *law* – Laura Norder, as it's sometimes described. When I was presenting *English Now* on

BBC Radio 4, I was sent each week all the letters from complaining listeners. They do notice tiny points of usage, and professional presenters know they do, so if a postbag or email inbox of criticism is to be avoided, the danger points need to be anticipated.

But the operative word is '*try* to remember'. With the best will in the world, it isn't possible to remember everything. Switching the audience context now from age to gender: I recall a university talk I gave once, in the 1970s, where a woman left in evident disgust at a certain point. I wondered what I had said. In the coffee break I saw her and asked her. It turned out to have been my use of the phrase *man in the street*, in its sense of 'ordinary person'. It was a time when feminism was in its ascendancy – but I knew that, and thought I'd been doing quite well in respecting the evolving climate in which such usages as gender-neutral pronouns were replacing male-orientated ones (as in *Doctors should ask their patients* instead of *A doctor should ask his patient*). But I hadn't even noticed *man in the street*. Idioms are always harder to control.

Old or young, male or female, experts or neophytes . . . This third category of audience probably raises more problems than any of the others, because it applies to any topic where speakers are talking to those who are not in their peer group. The risk is to forget the audience's innocent ignorance of your subject by using jargon that goes over their heads. Jargon is the specialist lexicon that belongs to a subject. It is invaluable in its original setting, as it expresses technical notions with a precision and mutuality of understanding among its practitioners that couldn't possibly be achieved in everyday language. But to use such vocabulary with people who don't share this background is a serious misjudgement.

You need to perform a kind of translation exercise. Anyone who wants to talk about their subject eloquently to a general audience has to learn to translate the vocabulary of their world into everyday terms. Popularization can therefore be an uncomfortable experience, until you get used to it, because you realize that everyday vocabulary expresses only part of the content that your technical vocabulary does. Eloquence, in such a context, is always dealing in half-truths. The trick is to work out which half of the truth to tell, so that you keep a balance between not alienating your audience and doing no disservice to your subject. Deciding what not to say – which details to leave out – is just as much a part of eloquence as deciding what to include.

All of this amounts to an apparently simple principle: you need to know who you're speaking to, as this will influence the way you speak. And this means seeing your audience as people with interests, attitudes, concerns, worries … In a word, you have to be sensitive to your listeners' *mood*.

What mood are they in? Is there something likely to be on all of their minds, such as a national disaster, or the death of a famous person? A flippant remark which might go down well on a light-hearted occasion could become a failure when everyone is feeling sombre. If a general election is approaching, a humorous reference to the main political leaders will very likely be appreciated (unless you're in a country where such remarks are likely to land you in jail). If you're talking early on the last day of a conference, and everyone has been up late partying the night before, be cautious: an over-enthusiastic presentation can make heads hurt (assuming the party-goers have bothered to get up to listen to you).

It's also important to be aware of what the audience has already experienced, if you are one of a string of speakers. There's a pecking order when it comes to eloquence. However eloquent you think you are, there will be someone who is more so. If you're talking at a conference – or at a wedding – who has been speaking before you? If speaker A has been rather serious, speaker B, coming on stage next, can gain from introducing some humour. And vice versa. A really eloquent speaker often gets a chair-person's accolade of: 'How do we follow that!' It poses a real challenge to the next speaker on the agenda. And if that happens to be you, there is only one principle: don't compete. Be yourself.

Most conference organizers know very well who the best speakers are, and will timetable them to 'start the conference off with a bang' or 'finish it with a bang'. But sometimes they get it wrong. I was once asked to be the last speaker at a 'Language Live' day arranged for A-level students. They'd scheduled the marvellous Guyanan poet, John Agard, before me. I could hear the students' loud and enthusiastic reactions to his dynamic performance from the green room a good distance away. When he'd finished, and it was my turn to speak, I had to find a way of getting the students to come down from the ceiling. I didn't succeed. That day ended not with a bang, but a whimper. And since then I have a principle: never follow a performance poet.

As with the rooms I described at the end of Chapter 5, you have to be prepared for the unexpected in your audience. A political heckle. A sudden illness or epileptic fit: 'Is there a doctor in the house?' doesn't happen only in theatres. A mobile phone going off. A sudden moment of unrestrained affection between two members of your audience. A loud snoring from the front row.

I advise speakers not to take these things personally. There's nothing in the notion of eloquence which says you will please all of the people all of the time. All you can do, in such circumstances, is try not to let the incident put you off. If it's a heckle, you can build it in to your speech. Audiences love it when a speaker turns the tables on a heckler. And they appreciate it if you give them a lead in a potentially awkward situation: if you show you're not embarrassed by the love-making or the snoring, they won't be either.

It doesn't bother me when someone falls asleep, because I've learned there's usually a good reason, such as jet lag. (If *all* the audience falls asleep, of course, then that's a different matter!) The sleeper can be cross or even dismissive about it: I recall one coming up to me in the coffee break, and unapologetically asking me what he'd missed. And on another occasion it was a sort of compliment. The sleeper's wife came up to me in the break and apologized for her husband falling asleep towards the end of my forty-five-minute talk. 'Mind you,' she said, 'you did very well. He normally falls asleep after ten minutes.'

Eloquence battles

I include rappers among my performance artists. I wouldn't want to speak after a rap genius like Akala either. Rappers provide the best evidence that eloquence can emerge from within anyone, and isn't restricted to the high styles of lecturers, politicians, and religious leaders.

Freestyle battle rapping illustrates the jaw-dropping possibilities. This is where rappers compete with each other by improvising rhyming lyrics, with the aim of defeating their opponents by using as much polysyllabic invention as they can muster. Judges or the audience, voting by acclamation, decide who has created the best sequence of exaggerated and sophisticated boasts, insults and put-downs.

This isn't something new in the story of language, as we saw in *bertsolari* (Chapter 2, p. 9), and it has a long history. In English, eloquent insult-exchanges in verse are found in Anglo-Saxon and medieval 'flyting' contests – a name that comes from an Old English verb *flitan* meaning 'dispute' or 'quarrel'.

Some virtuoso exchanges have been recorded, such as 'The Flyting of Dunbar and Kennedy' (*c*.1500), in which William Dunbar and Walter Kennedy swap character assassinations. The flavour of the piece is captured in this early salvo from Dunbar:

> Thow crop and rute of traitouris tressonable,
> The fathir and moder of murthour and mischeif,
> Dissaitfull tyrand, with serpentis tung, ynstable;
> Cuckald crawdoun [craven], cowart, and commoun theif . . . [11]

It goes on like this for 552 lines.

Flyting was always aggressive and cantankerous. But rap doesn't have to be a battle. It can simply be to delight listeners. Akala was once challenged to create a freestyle rap using the titles of Shakespeare plays. His twenty-seven-title piece, put together in ten minutes, was recorded eventually with the title 'Comedy Tragedy History'. Here's a flavour of it, an extract from verse 2:

> . . . I'm fire, things look dire,
> Better run like Pericles Prince of Tyre
> Off the scale, cold as a Winter's Tale
> Titus Andronicus was bound to fail
> So will you if Akala get at ya
> That's suicide like Anthony and Cleopatra . . .

But no written extract can ever do justice to the pace and timing of the vocal performance of an accomplished rapper.

7

Who am I talking to – abroad?

To see an audience closing its eyes doesn't always mean that your listeners are asleep. It may simply mean they're concentrating hard or wishing to avoid eye contact. In some cultures it's a well-established behaviour. I've talked to audiences (e.g. in Japan) where most of the people had their eyes closed most of the time. It's disturbing, if you're used to audiences who keep their eyes on you – as if each person is willing you to look back at them individually – and who give you lots of visual feedback.

Speaking abroad, to people with a different cultural or linguistic background, can seriously alter your delivery. They say humour doesn't travel. Nor, sometimes, does eloquence. Even if you and your audience all speak English, you need to be cautious. You may share the same language, but you don't share the same culture.

The contrast can manifest itself in all kinds of little ways, such as the colloquial expressions and idioms you use without thinking. Many of these depend for an understanding on a knowledge of local culture. I recall being in a seminar audience where a speaker from the USA was eloquently expounding his subject to an international group of teachers. He paused and asked if there were any questions. A participant asked one that evidently took him by surprise, because he was silent for a few moments before saying, 'Hmm, that was from out of left field.' And he paused again.

The person sitting next to me nudged me and whispered: 'What does that mean?' I whispered back: 'I've no idea.' The lecturer noticed the whispering. 'Is there a problem?' 'We don't know what "from out of left field" means,' I said. 'Huh?' he exclaimed. His face was a picture. It had never occurred to him that this common American expression, from baseball (as I later learned), would not be understood. He had to explain, and he didn't find it easy. Eloquent he wasn't. Apparently, the left part of the outfield is furthest from the first base, so that if the ball is hit in that direction the fielder has the longest distance to throw it back. The expression thus means 'unexpected' or 'out of the ordinary'. I thanked him, adding: 'You played that with a straight bat.' Another facial picture. 'Huh?'

My cricketing idiom was just as opaque to him as the baseball idiom had been to a Brit. We both learned something about each other's sporting cultures that day. But here's the point: after the interchange, the speaker was far less eloquent than before. He seemed to be checking himself mentally to ensure that he didn't use any more culturally loaded expressions. And in the bar afterwards, he acknowledged that this was exactly what he had been doing.

Cultural differences affect far more than individual words and phrases. They can influence the content and delivery of your speech. Some cultures want to hear hard facts, data, scholarly references (e.g. Germany, Scandinavia); some want a lot of personal background (e.g. Italy and other Romance-speaking countries); some value eloquence and a high style of speaking (e.g. those in the subcontinent of India); some value emotional content and personal enthusiasm (e.g. many Latin American countries); some emphasize solidarity with the audience, such as a shared educational or locality background (e.g. the USA); some like humour, light-heartedness, and self-effacement (e.g. Britain); some expect formality, with explicit respect paid to the chairperson and any patrons present (e.g. East Asian countries).

The protocol can count for everything. I once had to give a talk about one of my books in a large bookstore in Tokyo. I was asked to arrive in good time, to meet the staff. I turned up at the language section of the store, and found a sales assistant, who introduced me to the manager for that section. He then took me into a side room where I met the floor manager, the manager of the bookstore, and the bookstore owner. After tea and a well-attended talk, there was a period devoted to questions. I waited for one. None came.

To start things moving, I decided to ask a question of my own. I turned to the sales assistant and asked him which of my books was selling most at the moment. He thanked me for my question, and bowed to his manager, who thanked me for my question, and bowed to the floor manager, who thanked me and bowed to the store manager, who thanked me and bowed to the owner. The owner then made a statement about the impressive record of his store, and how many English-language books sold well in Japan, before finally turning to the sales assistant to ask him to answer my question.

The protocol can affect the audience's readiness to respond, and this can affect your ability to give eloquent answers in a Q&A session, or just generally in an informal discussion. Talking to a university audience in the Far East, I learned that it was highly unlikely that students would ask a question before their professors did. And even the professors might be reluctant, because, after all, what could asking a question mean? In Western cultures it usually means that the questioner wants to know more. It shows the speaker has been understood and that the questioner has been listening. Even if questioners fail to actually ask a question, but make a long-winded statement or adopt a contrary position, it's a kind of compliment to the speaker. It shows they've been intellectually stimulated.

This isn't always so in other cultures. Asking a question can be thought of as an admission that you haven't been listening properly, or that you have some mental limitation in your ability to understand. To ask a question in public is to lose face. Worse, it might be interpreted as an insult to the speaker. If I ask you a question it means you haven't been very clear in what you said. (None of this applies in private, one-to-one interactions. After my bookstore talk, where there were no further questions at all in that Q&A session, I was besieged by people wanting to ask me a question.)

The cultural differences can impact on the eloquence of our speech in many ways, but we should never underestimate their importance. Take the way we name people, for instance. In some countries it would be considered friendly and polite to refer to the chair or the sponsor by their first names, and they would respond to you likewise. In others, only a full title (such as 'Professor Doctor So-and-so') will do. At the Emirates Airline Festival of Literature in 2015, held in Dubai, it was notable (to me as a first-time outsider) how all references to the country's ruler were made in full, sometimes with his role explicitly stated: His Highness Sheikh Mohammed Bin Rashid Al Maktoum, Vice President and Prime Minister of the United Arab Emirates and Ruler of Dubai. One might hear this several times in a speech.

It pays to obtain as much cultural awareness as possible in advance of a visit, and these days there are several excellent sources of information available. Foreign audiences appreciate a speaker who has some knowledge of their country, and who can refer to home-grown personalities in the same field. But it's important to keep that awareness up to date. Don't refer to the local experts you mentioned three years ago without checking that something tragic hasn't happened to them. International organizations usually have a lot of experience to share. And there's nothing wrong with gaining some insight by talking to a friend, neighbour, or local shopkeeper who comes from the country you're about to visit.

Sometimes a lack of cultural awareness of your audience can lead to real problems. The organization that invites you to speak should alert you to any potential pitfalls. When the British Council first invited me to speak in Arab countries, it sent me an invaluable briefing about the kind of thing that would not go down well – no references to Israel, for example, or to Hebrew, otherwise half my audience might walk out. I've no idea how widespread this reaction is, but it's always wise to err on the safe side. Many countries have taboo topics, especially if there has been a recent confrontation with some other country. In the 1990s, just after the Balkan wars of independence, a talk in Croatia which mentioned examples of good practice in Serbia would not have gone down well, and of course vice versa.

It also pays to learn something about typical audience responses. You expect immediate noisy, hand-clapping, whistling applause at the end of your speech? Then be prepared for cultures where approval is expressed by a drumming of hands on desks (as in Germany) or a low-key hum (as in some Far Eastern countries). What would be considered 'polite applause' in Britain can be the approval norm in some countries. Also be prepared for responses that mean different things. Whistling can mean approval – or disapproval. Giggling can mean delight – or embarrassment. Want a standing ovation after an eloquent speech? It depends where you are. Standing ovations are culture-bound too, even in English-speaking countries – almost *de rigueur* in the USA, especially in politics, much less so in Britain, and highly unusual in Australia.

Knowing a few phrases in the home language especially helps to establish rapport with an audience, but it's important to get the pronunciation right, especially if mentioning a person's name. I've heard many stories of a mispronounced name sending an audience into fits of laughter or an embarrassed silence because the speaker has inadvertently turned the name into a rude word. On the other hand, a well-pronounced foray into the home language can reap dividends.

I was once giving a talk on Shakespeare's language to an audience of English teachers in Toruń, Poland, and roped in Ben to say the quotations for me. We decided to use a running gag, with Ben the actor – now having an audience in front of him – wanting to recite 'To be, or not to be'. He would at intervals interrupt what I was saying, step forward and say that famous soliloquy's opening line, but I would tell him off and stop him saying anything further. Then, at the very end of the talk, the plan was that I would allow him, at last, to do it.

The joke worked well, and the audience enjoyed the moments of interruption, sympathizing with poor Ben. So when, at the end, I offered him the stage he got a round of applause. But unbeknown to me, Ben had earlier that day been in a local bookstore, found the speech in Polish translation, and had learned the opening line in Polish, with the help of the sales assistant. He stepped forward and said '*Być albo nie być – oto jest pytanie*'. He got a standing ovation. And ever since, when I meet people who were at that talk, what they remember is that final moment. One called it 'the to-be-or-not-to-be talk'. My part in it – the preceding forty-five minutes of eloquence – was as if it had never been.

The Polish audience consisted of teachers of English, so there was no need for translation. For general audiences, if you're giving your speech in English, many countries will want to have it translated. There are two main systems: simultaneous and successive. In simultaneous translation, the interpreter is sitting in a booth and those members of your audience who need help are using headphones. Note that *simultaneous* doesn't mean what it seems to mean. There's an inevitable lag between the time you say something and the time the translated version reaches the ears of the headphone-wearers. It may be anything from a second or so to several seconds. Usually the lag is of no consequence, but if you've made a successful humorous remark, bear in mind that the initial laugh from those not using headphones will be followed after an interval by another laugh from those who are. It can be quite off-putting in the middle of your next (serious) sentence to find an apparently irrelevant laugh suddenly emanating from the audience. It will pay you to pause a little longer than normal before continuing, to give everyone time to get the joke.

I find it's always worthwhile to meet the interpreter in advance – or interpreters, for the task of simultaneous translation is intense and tiring, and they often work a shift system. (The same principle applies if you're being interpreted into a sign language for deaf people.) If you have a broad regional accent, it gives them time to acclimatize to it. And they appreciate it if you draw attention to any points of unusual content or delivery, especially if you're going to be using difficult or archaic vocabulary (as in some literary quotations) or slang. If your speech is written down, they will be greatly aided by seeing a copy in advance. If your speech is spontaneous, let them know of any effects that are likely to take them by surprise or even be untranslatable. In one of my talks, for example, I illustrate various facial expressions, gestures, and body postures, and there are moments of silence. In another, I illustrate various English accents. Knowing about these in advance allows the translator time to decide how to alert the listeners to what is going on.

In successive translation, the interpreter is usually working alongside you, visible to the audience. You say something, and it's translated. Then you say something else, and that's translated. And so on. No headphones are needed in this case. But a strategy needs to be agreed in advance. To work effectively, you need to speak in stretches that fall comfortably within your translator's auditory memory. If you speak for too long without a pause, only the gist of what you say will be translated. On the other hand, you don't want to pause too often, as this can so disrupt the flow of ideas that it can be difficult for people to follow what you're saying. It's a tricky balance, and few speakers maintain it with ease.

It's virtually impossible to be eloquent, or be perceived as eloquent, in these situations. Your delivery is now in the hands of someone whose remit is simply to translate efficiently, and you have no way of knowing or controlling the extent to which they are conveying your individual linguistic choices to the audience. Also, the time you have available to speak is now cut in half, so that will have consequences for the way you organize your thoughts. All you can do in such situations, is – once again – be yourself, and speak in your normal style to those in the audience who don't need the translator. Some features of your personal eloquence will cross the language barrier. And many of the people using the interpreter will actually have a limited knowledge of English, so they'll be half-listening to you in any case.

An unusual situation occurs when the interpreter is actually more eloquent than you are. I remember watching a woman interpreting a speech into American Sign Language, and doing so with such panache that everyone had their eyes on her and not on the speaker. And once, when I was giving a talk to a university audience in a South American country where a popular revolution was taking place, I received repeated applause when my banal sentences about linguistics were successively translated into Spanish by an eloquent interpreter who (I found out later) kept referring to me as a man who had come all the way from Britain to support the revolutionary cause. Borrowed eloquence can, it seems, make you a local hero.

Teach me, believe me, move me

The different cultural expectations described in Chapter 6 often reflect the aims of public speaking recognized by the orators of ancient Greece and Rome, prioritizing them differently. According to Aristotle, you can persuade an audience in three ways:

- *logos* ('word') – persuasion through the use of reason, respecting the role of evidence, logic, clarity, coherence;
- *ethos* ('character') – persuasion using the character of the speaker, identified through reputation, expertise, credibility, personality;
- *pathos* ('suffering') – persuasion by appealing to the emotions, arousing sympathy, stimulating the imagination, identifying with traditions and beliefs.

A talk on, say, English accents would begin differently in each case.

- in a logos approach, start by defining what an accent is, and showing a map of accent areas in Britain;
- in an ethos approach, start by telling the audience what books I've written on accents, or where I've studied accents;
- in a pathos approach, start by telling a story about people who lost their jobs because of their accents, or ask the audience whether they pronounce certain words the same as me.

The most eloquent speeches make effective use of all three elements, and this is where preparation begins.

8

What to say?

So, you know how long you've got to speak, where you'll be speaking, and who your audience is. Now to the main challenges:

- what to say,
- when to say it,
- how to say it.

The first is sometimes felt to be so obvious that it is taken for granted. It shouldn't be.

If you've been asked to give a talk, the theme is usually clear in advance. Either you've been asked to speak on a particular topic (e.g. your recent trip abroad, your hobby, your latest research, the launch of a new product), or the topic is one that convention requires you to make your primary focus (e.g. an anniversary, the Gospel of the day, political party policy, the bridegroom). Occasionally, as with many after-dinner speeches, the invitation is wide open: 'talk about whatever you like'. That doesn't mean what it appears to mean. You always have to bear in mind the nature of the occasion and the interests of the audience.

And their familiarity with your subject matter. This is the jargon demon that I briefly discussed in Chapter 6. You may be able to talk eloquently about the history of racing-car engines, but if your audience has no idea what torque is, or a variable intake trumpet, and can't expand abbreviations such as RPM (revolutions per minute) and FIA (Fédération Internationale de l'Automobile), you may well find that it simply isn't possible to give the talk you want. The point applies to any subject, and not just to technical ones. If you're giving a wedding speech, the jargon is now domestic in character – family slang, and repeated allusions to an infamous relative such as 'Auntie Grace'. Only one side of the audience will know who Auntie Grace is – and maybe not even all of those.

If you're not sure what to say, you may well turn to a guide for help. Reading a popularization on your subject can give you clues about how to make your subject accessible to a general audience. And there are any number of books or websites telling you how to make a good speech at a wedding. They can be helpful, because they tell you what points you need to address (who to thank, who to toast . . .). But it's wise not to follow them too slavishly, such as by using jokes that the source thinks will go down well. Jokes tend to go the rounds, and the assembly is likely to have heard them before.

Some topics are 'one-off', in the sense that you'll never have to speak about them again. You'll never say again what you say at a book launch, a golden wedding anniversary party, or a funeral. Others are reproducible. You give an eloquent talk about your trip to Africa to a local club, and suddenly everyone wants to hear it. You're asked to another group, then another. And because the audiences are different, you can repeat yourself. Indeed, there may be an expectation that you repeat yourself, especially if your story of nearly being eaten by a crocodile has travelled in the meantime.

'We must have you back.' That's the accolade of eloquence. You've pleased your audience to such an extent that they want to hear you again. Sometimes they're saying it just for politeness' sake. But if you think they mean it, then make a note of what you talked about. Because, if a second invitation does arrive, it's remarkable how quickly you find you've forgotten what you talked about the first time you addressed that group, especially if you give several talks each year. You don't want to repeat yourself. No amount of eloquence can survive the bored reaction: 'We heard all that last time.' Political speakers have to fight against this during every campaign. They have to repeat the same message, but in such a way that it comes across freshly.

Having said that, if you spoke spontaneously the first time you gave a particular talk (rather than reading your text), then obviously there will be numerous points of difference between the occasions. Time has passed, so novel observations are bound to enter in. And it's worth remembering the point I made in Chapter 1, that real eloquence is a source of delight in itself, so if people are enjoying themselves they'll be prepared to make allowances for repeated subject matter. They may even look forward to it. You can enjoy each new production of *Hamlet* even if you know the play backwards. The trick, as every actor and director knows, is to find something new to add to the familiar content. It's the same with public speaking.

'Something new' also has to be interpreted with reference to others, as well as to yourself. If the occasion is one of a series – such as speaking at the annual dinner of a society – it's worthwhile finding out what topic your predecessor addressed the previous year. Once again, you don't want to be repetitive, unless of course you deliberately intend your take on that topic to contrast with what went before. Sometimes finding out about previous speakers is easy, as the speech (or a summary of it) may have been published in the society's newsletter. If not, I always ask. People have long memories when it comes to special occasions, and eloquence stays in the mind. Another comment you don't want to elicit: 'Wasn't as good as last year's.'

'What to say' should always be thought of, initially, in relation to the three Aristotelian methods that I outlined in Interlude 7, because they're applicable to all public-speaking situations, not just those where your intention is to persuade people to agree with you. Whatever your intention – whether or not it is, like the BBC, 'to inform, educate, and entertain' – you're faced with the same task as those whose remit is to present their case. You need to get the audience on your side so that they're ready to listen to what you want to say. Logos, ethos, pathos: which is it to be?

In my view, ethos is paramount. The audience needs to know who you are. I don't mean your role or reputation. That's taken for granted. If you're a best man at a wedding, everyone knows who you are, in the sense that they know your relationship to the groom. If you're speaking at a literary festival or a conference, your reputation has preceded you. As the chairperson regularly says, 'This is someone who really needs no introduction.' Knowing who you are means much more than that. People often say, 'It's nice to put a face to the name.' They want to put a voice to the name too. It is the powerful meaning behind Socrates' maxim: 'Speak that I may see thee.'

Opening remarks are critical in this respect. First impressions always count. Eloquent speakers typically open their speech with a personal remark or story, and personal reflections recur throughout. At the end, listeners feel they have come to know them a bit. We feel we've taken away a piece of that person. 'Be yourself?' Eloquent speakers have indeed 'been themselves'.

Eloquence varies in its consistency. When we say that someone spoke eloquently, we don't mean the speaker was eloquent in exactly the same way throughout the entire presentation. There may have been passages where the speech was quite pedestrian. We may only recall flashes of eloquence, but these are enough to colour the recollection as a whole. They are the bits of the speech we remember, and tell others about when they ask 'What did he/she say?' The opening of the speech is one of those special moments.

This is felt to be such an important element of eloquence that some guides to public speaking make it a mantra: start with a story. It's one of the most powerful recommendations from those who have studied the hugely successful online TED presentations. Chapter 2 of *Talk Like TED*, by Carmine Gallo, is headed 'Master the Art of Storytelling', and the theme is taken up. 'Stories are central to who we are.' 'Tell stories to reach people's hearts and minds.' The stories may be about you (ethos) or about someone else (pathos), but their function is the same. The chapter ends with the words: 'Stories illustrate, illuminate, and inspire.'[12] To which I would add: and also individuate, or perhaps better, incarnate, in its sense of 'make yourself manifest'.

I always start a talk with a story. Sometimes it's no more than a personal reflection about the last time I was in that part of the country. It may relate to something the chairperson has just said by way of introduction. It may be about the title of the talk. It needn't take long. For instance, whenever I'm asked to give a lecture on 'The Future of Englishes', I begin by telling a story about how sometimes advance publicity in the press gets the title wrong. Having assumed that no such word as 'Englishes' exists in the English language, the talk is reported as being on 'The Future of English'. It takes only a minute to tell it, and an audience of language teachers and students is quick to see the irony in the situation.

At least, that is what I hope they see. Do they get the point? There's a second reason for beginning with a story, and that is to gauge the response temperature of the audience. The story may have little or nothing to do with the 'meat' of the presentation that is to follow; but simply by telling it, you allow your listeners (along with any interpreters) to get used to your voice and your manner of presentation. If this is at all idiosyncratic, it enables them to tune in to your style. And – a basic but crucial point – it gives you a chance to check that everyone can hear you while saying something that's relatively unimportant.

In return, you get a sense of their mood and expectations. If it's a non-specialist audience where most speak English as a foreign language, you can get an immediate sense of their level of comprehension. If they evidently enjoy the story, your level must be right. If they look blank, or embarrassed, or start muttering to each other, or even (I've seen it happen) take out their mobile phone to look up one of your words in an online dictionary, you've overestimated. I often change my style – perhaps speaking less colloquially, or less humorously – if the initial reaction isn't what I hoped for.

The story may even be about the way you look. My beard has been the source of innumerable anecdotes, but most speakers have some sort of personal idiosyncrasy that they can use to good effect. Your physical appearance may actually be something temporary. I remember having to give a lecture in Egypt to an audience of English teachers and students, on behalf of the British Council. The day before, our host had taken us on a trip to see some of the lesser known pyramids to the south of Cairo. 'We go into that one,' he said, pointing to a door halfway up the side of one of them. Up we went, and then discovered that to get down to the centre of the pyramid you had to follow a steep, stepped, narrow shaft, just a few feet square. To move along it you had to crouch down almost on all fours and move yourself along, step by step, crablike. When we got to the centre, we were able to stand in the burial chamber and reflect on the thousands of tons of rock above us. Then it was back up again, crablike in reverse now.

I staggered back to the car, and to the hotel, woke up next day, and found I could hardly move. Walking along to breakfast was a major enterprise. I approached a step in the lobby and realized that my legs would not respond to my brain's instructions to lift each one. I shuffled sideways up the step, holding onto the wall. My lecture was later that morning. I got myself into the chair next to the podium while my host introduced me, then realized I could not get up. I struggled out of the chair, while the audience watched in some puzzlement, and clutched the podium at an angle while I told my story of what had happened. Puzzlement turned to amusement. They understood my problem, as many had suffered as I had. This was pathos at its best. I think I could have recited the telephone directory that day and they wouldn't have minded.

People love to hear stories, so starting with one shows your audience you're human, not as fearsome as they thought you might be. It helps to relax them. They become more receptive. And there's a second reason for starting with a story. It fits perfectly with what we know about the way listeners pay attention.

It ain't what you say . . .

To my mind, the best definition of delivery is to adapt the old jazz lyric that Ella Fitzgerald used to sing back in 1939, followed by many others: 'T'ain't what you do, it's the way that you do it.' When it comes to eloquence, 'T'ain't what you say, it's the way that you say it.' That's what gets results.

Nor should the lyric stop there. It's not only the way that you say it, but the way that you look when you say it. I'll talk about that later. And, more important than either of these, it's the time when you say it. That comes next.

9

When do you say it?

Talks and speeches are usually measured in minutes, these days. The Castro and Gaddafi marathons I described in Interlude 4 are exceptions. TED talks are no more than eighteen minutes. After-dinner speeches may be twenty or thirty minutes (people want their money's worth, especially if the speaker is an expensive celebrity). Lectures and conference presentations are typically forty-five minutes to an hour. Sermons tend to be half that, but there's a great deal of variation, and some congregations feel short-changed if their pastor doesn't keep them listening for the best part of an hour. Radio and television interviews are usually three or four minutes. Top-of-the-hour radio talks can be under one minute.

To be eloquent, you have to make the best possible use of those minutes. The content of your speech needs to be structured so that it comes across most effectively in the time available. And for this to happen, you need to recognize that, from your audience's point of view, the minutes you have at your disposal don't all work in the same way. Some minutes are much more important than others. It's all to do with the way listeners pay attention.

Everyone knows what it's like not to pay attention. You're listening to someone talking, and then you suddenly realize you've stopped listening. Your mind has wandered. It can happen anywhere, even in a conversation ('Sorry . . . what was that you just said?'), but it's especially common when you're not being interactive, and just listening to a speech. Anything can trigger the distraction – an uncomfortable chair, noticeable room temperature, soporific lighting . . .

You don't mean to do it. Anyone who takes the trouble to go to hear a speaker, or even pay to hear a speaker, wants to attend to what the speaker has to say. Even if you have no choice but to listen – as with school students when there's a visiting speaker, or staff attendees instructed to go to a marketing meeting – you want to take something away from the occasion. Nobody likes to think they've wasted their time. So it can be quite annoying when you realize you haven't taken in a word the speaker has been saying for . . . how long? It's usually only a few seconds, but it might be minutes, and if something important has been said during that mind-wandering episode, it can disturb your grasp of the rest of the speech.

This is going to happen to your audience, no matter how eloquent you are. Nobody is exempt. Even the most eloquent speakers can lose their listeners some of the time. Eloquence, as I said in the previous chapter, varies in its consistency. But you can lose your listeners even if you are supremely consistent. Keeping up with an eloquent speaker can actually be more effortful than keeping up with a pedestrian one. There's more to listen to, more to engage with, more to enjoy. Listening isn't just hearing. Hearing is a passive state; listening is active – hearing with attention. And it can be tiring.

So, if this is the normal state of affairs when listening to a presentation, the wise public speaker will take steps to minimize the effects of inattention. The really eloquent speaker is the one who makes the task of listening as easy as possible. And that means being aware of the factors that promote inattention. Some are outside the speaker's control – such as the external distractions I described at the end of Chapter 5 – but others are manageable.

The chief factor is attention span – the amount of time you can attend to something before your mind starts to wander. It's actually quite difficult to measure, and many experiments have been carried out, using a variety of methods, to determine what it could be. Researchers might ask people to fill in a question-naire about how much they remember of the speech they've just heard, to see the points when inattention crept in. Or they might monitor the number of notes students make during a lecture. Or they might ask the attendees to send a signal, using some sort of button-pressing technology, each time they felt their attention was slipping during a talk. Results don't always agree, but some useful general points have emerged, often summarized in the form of a graph showing how people listen over a period of time.

Let's take a presentation of thirty or forty minutes. A popular belief is that your level of attention will be high at the outset and will gradually decline over time, so that at the end you're hardly listening. That graph would look like this:

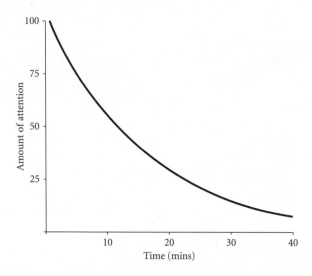

The research studies show that in fact your attention varies more like this:

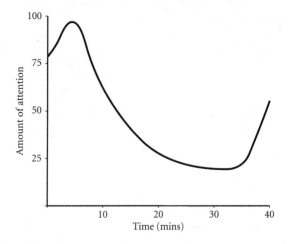

What this graph says is that, at the very beginning of a talk, people are quite attentive, because of the novelty and freshness of the situation, but they take a minute or so to 'settle in' before their attention peaks. It then declines steadily until just before the end of the speech, when it begins to rise again. It suggests that listeners want to take something away with them. (The graph assumes that you've kept to time. My story in Chapter 4 is a reminder that overrunning can destroy any normal pattern.)

That isn't the end of the attention story, but the graph as it stands certainly sends a speaker two very important messages:

- Don't say anything really important at the very begin-ning; wait a couple of minutes, and fill those minutes by saying something trivial, or – see the previous chapter – by telling a story.
- Do say something really important during the last few minutes, such as a recapitulation of your main points, or a restatement of a critical message.

The steady decline in the middle of the graph is misleading. In reality, attention turns out to be a series of peaks and troughs at fairly regular intervals. Listeners who are trying to pay attention will find their concentration slipping every so often, and then regain it, often by an effort of will. At worst, this can amount to the tell-tale downward fluttering of the eyelids and the sudden head-jerk, especially common in a room that has no natural daylight. Or it can be a wakeful but equally distracting tour of the audience ('There's Derek ... haven't seen him for ages ...', 'That's a rather nice-looking jacket ...'), domestic reflections ('Did I remember to feed the cat?', 'I wonder where Mary is right now ...'), a review of the conference programme, or a search for new messages on a laptop or mobile phone.

Researchers have tried to make precise what 'every so often' means. It's usually claimed that there's an attention trough every ten or fifteen minutes. People, situations, topics, and speakers are so different that it's impossible to generalize about the extent of the attention loss, but troughs at regular intervals there will definitely be. A typical attention graph would look more like this:

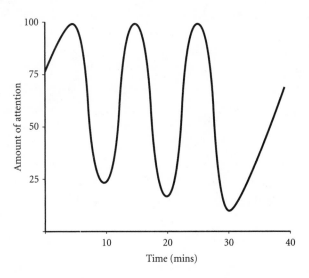

So this is another guideline for speakers: if some sort of attention loss occurs roughly every ten minutes, they can adapt their speech to work within these spans. Many do this instinctively. They develop a sense of how much material their audience can take, and introduce an information lull – which isn't silence, but a signal to everyone that they can relax for a while. How they fill the lull varies. It can be another story. It can be a reference to something that is happening in the outside world (Chapter 5: HOWZAT?). It can be a moment for people to talk to each other – to discuss the point that was just made (a frequent strategy used by teacher trainers).

Speakers often use these moments as signposts. One pointer looks back at what has already been said; the other looks forward.

> I've talked about A and B . . . now I want to talk about C and D.

Recapitulation and anticipation. Here's a real example from a talk I gave on the endangered languages of the world.

> [after two minutes] . . . so today I'm going to begin by reporting how many languages in the world are in danger of extinction. Then I'll talk about why. And then what if anything can be done to reverse the decline . . .
> [after fifteen minutes] . . . so there are the facts. Half the languages of the world are going to die out before this century is over. It's an unprecedented situation, and it raises the obvious question: Why has this happened? There are three main reasons . . .
> [after thirty minutes] . . . Natural disasters, linguistic genocide, globalization. These are three powerful processes, and they are still with us. So, is there anything we can do about language death? And should we be doing something about it? . . .

Then, fifteen minutes later, the talk ended with a restatement of the three subtopics.

The same strategy of introducing a lull can be used even when there are different speakers. My son Ben used to be host of conference days called 'Poetry Live'. Large numbers of school students would come to a major venue and hear a range of talks or readings from the poets they would be studying in school, such as Simon Armitage and Carol Ann Duffy. It was an unusual and intensive situation for the students, to be sitting and listening to high-profile talks, often on seats whose proper-ties would score low on any comfort graph. There were breaks every ninety minutes or so, of course, but that's a long time to keep students attentive, especially after lunch in the afternoon – a sleepy digesting period which many speakers fear, whatever the age of the audience. So Ben would get them to do a Mexican wave across the hall after the first afternoon talk and before the last session. The accompanying teachers looked a bit uncomfortable, but the students loved it. And it did its job. Briskly standing up and down a few times gave them a fresh span of attentional life, and carried them through to the end of the day.

That story has a sad ending, as on one occasion a teacher complained and the organizers asked Ben to stop. Health and safety, I suppose. But any change in activity can produce the same results, physical or otherwise. I've never tried a Mexican wave myself – the effect on a U3A (University of the Third Age) audience might be catastrophic – but I have tried other things. If I'm on my own for a Shakespeare talk (without actors to help perform the extracts) I find a good attention-replenishing task is to get the audience to do some performing in unison. For example, there's a moment in *The Tempest* when Stephano and Trinculo find themselves on Prospero's island. They've taken charge of Caliban, Prospero's slave, and made him so drunk that he begins to dream of freedom, saying:

'Ban, 'Ban, Cacaliban
Has a new master: get a new man.

The first line can confuse students, who try to say it as poetry.
But it's actually a triumphant chant. So I get them to shout it
out in the manner of a crowd attending a football match, beating
out the syllables:

'BAN, 'BAN, CAcaliBAN
HAS a new MAster: GET a new MAN!

After doing that a few times, any lethargy disappears. It's the
vocal equivalent of a Mexican wave. I like to introduce such a
change of pace every ten minutes or so. It doesn't just energize
the audience. It energizes me.

Knowing about attention spans also makes my life easier
when it comes to planning a talk. If there's going to be a lull
every ten minutes, then it makes me think in a modular way. If
I have to speak for forty-five minutes, then I know I have four
modules to fill, each roughly ten minutes long. It's a hugely
useful first step, when dealing with a theme that has a dozen
important issues all clamouring to be made, to know that, from
an audience's point of view, they will find it easiest if you focus
on four, and no more.

There are some tricks of eloquence that can allow you a bit
more flexibility, such as adding a fresh story or doing something
unexpected. Experienced speakers can bend and break the ten-
minute guideline. But if you're new to public speaking, or at all
nervous about it, it's a good strategy to take it as a rule. If your
talk is going to be thirty minutes long, you have three modules
to fill. If twenty, two. And if five or ten, just one. You don't need
to worry about a change of pace if you're giving a five-minute
speech at a wedding. But you do need to keep your audience's
interest nonetheless. How is it done?

Strings of pearls

There are occasions when everyone is so excited and fired up about what is happening that normal notions of attention span are simply irrelevant. Nobody is suggesting that, when you're watching a fast-moving game, such as a football match, your attention is going to slip every ten minutes. The excitement over what's taking place, plus your personal interest in the outcome, plus the vocal rapport with fellow spectators, gives you a buzz that keeps your attention focused throughout.

It's the same with any speaking situation where there's a special kind of commitment present, and people hang on to every word. They don't need an ice-breaking introduction, as described in Chapter 8; a simple greeting will do. And they're able to pay attention over long stretches of time. As a result, the usual pattern of recapitulation and anticipation isn't needed. Rather, the structure of the speech is better likened to a string of pearls, with some pearls bigger than others. It is a sequence of related and telling points, each one of which energizes the audience in some way.

We see this structure in speeches at religious rallies, award-giving ceremonies, and company presentations leading up to the climactic moment when a new product is revealed. We see it at weddings and funerals. And above all, we see it in the political victory speech.

When President Obama made his 'Yes we can' victory speech in 2008, I was watching, and was so impressed by the eloquence that I spent the next day analysing it for a post on my blog. The next chapters describe what I found, but in such a way that the points can be applied to all other public-speaking situations.

10

How do they do it? The memory game

I would never be comfortable starting a chapter with a long *if*-clause, like this:

> If there is one topic in the study of eloquence that authors have dealt with more than any other ...

It's asking a lot of a reader. You have to keep all this in your head before you get to the point, whatever that's going to be. And with two such clauses, the strain on your memory is even greater:

> If there is one topic in the study of eloquence that authors have dealt with more than any other, that speakers have always found to be one of the greatest difficulties to overcome ...

'Get on with it,' you'll be thinking. And if I went on like this for a third time, you might well decide to go and read something else.

> If there is one topic in the study of eloquence that authors have dealt with more than any other, that speakers have always

found to be one of the greatest difficulties to overcome, that audiences the world over have found effective ...

You *might* stay with me. At least when you're reading you can read at your own pace, and reread if necessary. But you can't listen at your own pace, or relisten when you hear something for the first time. So I wouldn't expect to hear a long *if*-clause at the beginning of a speech. Or an *if*-clause followed by two more subordinate clauses, making a total of forty-one words before getting to the point.

But that is what we got, when Obama began his victory speech to an audience of around a quarter of a million at Grant Park in Chicago on 4 November 2008. As he launched into it, I turned to my wife and said, 'He'll never do it!' I thought he would be lucky if he was able to round it off neatly after the first comma. Yet, after forty-one words and a four-word punchline, he got huge applause. Here is what he said, after an initial greeting ('Hello, Chicago!'):

If there is anyone out there who still doubts that America is a place where all things are possible, who still wonders if the dream of our founders is alive in our time, who still questions the power of our democracy, tonight is your answer.

I suppose, given the occasion, he could have said anything at all and got a huge cheer. I imagine a short, punchy one-liner ('We did it!') would have elicited just as loud a response. But that isn't an eloquent opening. Anyone could say such a thing, and eloquence – recall Chapter 1 – is going beyond the ordinary. Obama's first full sentence was certainly extra-ordinary.

How did it work? How can you get people to process forty-one words easily? By following some basic rules of eloquence. You first have to think of each sentence, or each major part of a sentence, as being a chunk of information that has to be understood. This is why grammar – essentially, the study of sentence structure – is so important, and why I need to use terms such as *clause* to explain what happens when people are eloquent. Clauses are the main means we have of organizing complex thoughts. Each clause has a verb as its focal point – a word that typically expresses an action or a relationship or a state of mind – and its function is to show how the other elements in the clause relate to each other. Some sentences have just one clause. (That's an example.) Others, such as Obama's opener, have several.

Here's the basic structure of that first sentence, with the verbs in bold:

> If there **is** anyone out there
> who still **doubts**
> > that America **is** a place
> > where all things **are** possible,
> who still **wonders**
> > if the dream of our founders **is** alive in our time,
> who still **questions** the power of our democracy,
> tonight **is** your answer.

As soon as it's laid out like this, you begin to see the artistry of the speech writers. It shows three properties:

- there's an evident parallelism with *who still*,
- the inner complexity of the sentence is organized into three main chunks,
- the chunks are easy to process in listeners' working memory.

Each of these is a well-established strategy. Indeed, you can't be eloquent without them. So, before going into Obama's speech further, I'll describe how they work, starting with the memory issue, for that one underpins the others.

George Miller, an American psychologist, once proposed 'the magical number seven, plus or minus two'. That's the title of a paper he published in *Psychological Review* in 1956. It had the subtitle 'Some Limits on our Capacity for Processing Information', and it stimulated a huge amount of research into the way memory works. Most young adults, it was claimed, find seven chunks of information the most they can handle at a time, before they lose track of what's being said. For some, the limit is five chunks. Others can handle up to nine.

Later research modified the claims, but retained the principle. It became clear that the span of your working memory is a variable, affected by all kinds of factors, such as your age, your knowledge of the subject being talked about, and – in the case of speech – the words you choose and how they're used in a sentence. It's easier to retain short words than long ones, for instance. And a lot depends on the way the words are organized grammatically and how they're emphasized. For speech, the number of chunks that can be easily handled is better captured by the formula 'five, plus or minus one'.

This may all sound a bit technical, so it would be good, at this point, to prove the existence of this processing limit to yourself. It's easy to do. You can try it out on someone else (or get them to try it out on you). You simply ask them to repeat what you say, and to note the point when they find it difficult to remember what you've said. Start with random monosyllabic digits, saying each one as a separate item, with the same pitch movement:

3

6, 2

9, 5, 8

4, 2, 3, 5

9, 3, 6, 8, 2

6, 4, 1, 9, 2, 5

2, 5, 3, 8, 6, 9, 4

Most people sense a difficulty when the sequence reaches five, and become hesitant, omit items, or get the order wrong. Some can't get beyond this. I try this out with audiences sometimes, and get them to chant the numbers together. They shout out confidently in unison to begin with, but performance begins to straggle when I reach six. If I lengthen the words, the deterioration starts earlier:

14
17, 13
18, 15, 19

and so on.

And you can imagine the result when I use really long words:

consequence
readiness, engineering
habituation, evanescence, corporation, exactitude . . .

Of course, such tasks are a long way from speech reality. In real speech, we introduce all kinds of tricks enabling us to hold stretches of language easily in our memory. And the most important is grammar. We don't speak words in isolation. We put them into sentences, and the rules of grammar help us see the relationship between the words and to remember them. Grammar enables us to process our thoughts comfortably.

But it can't do it alone. In writing, we need graphic clues to help us read and write comfortably. That's why punctuation developed, along with other features of layout. In speech, we need auditory clues to help us speak and listen comfortably. That's the job of intonation (speech melody) and rhythm. Are you someone who gave up, in the repetition experiment, when you got to five or six spoken digits? You might well think, as a result, that you could never handle a sequence of eight. Yes you can.

All you have to do is group the digits into sets, and give each set its own intonation and rhythm. So you don't say them as 3 ... 6 ... 1 ... 5, but as 3615, with the emphasis on the 5 – just as you would say a telephone number. Now try that with eight digits: 3615 ... 8294. Look away now, and you'll remember it. If you asked someone for their number, and that is what they said, you'd be able to write it down quite easily.

So, to return to Obama. I'll now present his opening sentence as a series of intonation-plus-rhythm chunks, marking the main pauses. It looks like this:

> if there - is anyone out there --
> who still doubts - that America is a place where all things
>   are possible --
> who still wonders - if the dream of our founders is alive
>   in our time --
> who still questions - the power of our democracy --
> tonight is your answer.

Now to add up the information-carrying elements in each chunk. Omit the words whose job is solely to link these elements ('grammatical words', such as *if, a, the, in, is, where*). We end up with this:

anyone + out-there	2
still + doubts	2
America + place + all + things + possible	5
still + wonders	2
dream + founders + alive + time	4
still + questions	2
power + democracy	2
tonight + answer	2

This is comfortable processing, both for speaker and listener. And note that the longest sequence is less than it seems, because *things* is a semantically empty word. *All things* might have been replaced with *everything* without loss. That line is really only four chunks of serious information:

America + place + all-things + possible   4

In fact the demands on the listener are even less than the numbers suggest because of the structural parallelism: *still doubts . . . still wonders . . . still questions . . .* When a word is set up as part of a pattern, we don't need to devote any fresh processing energy to it the second time it occurs, or the third time. It's not 'new news' any more. And that allows us more energy to concentrate on the following verbs – *doubts . . . wonders . . . questions* – that are actually the heart of this sentence. It's these verbs that give a focus to the emotionally charged nouns that accompany them: *America, power, democracy,* and the echoes of earlier famous speeches – *founders* (Abraham Lincoln) and *dream* (Martin Luther King).

It's fascinating – well, it is if you're a linguist – to go through a speech like this and identify the processing chunks. And to note the occasional places where the speaker dares to deliver a chunk that goes beyond that. I'll take just the next two paragraphs to illustrate this, because they show how Obama carries on with his pattern of 'easy listening', daring to do something a bit more challenging at one point. Once again, I'll lay it out in rhythm units and totals, with each information element shown in bold:

It's the **answer told** by **lines** that **stretched**   6
    around **schools** and **churches**
in **numbers** this **nation** has **never seen**   4
by **people** who **waited three hours** and **four hours**   6
many for the **first time** in their **lives**   4

because they **believed** that this **time** must be **different** 3
that their **voices** could be that **difference**   2

It's the **answer spoken** by **young** and **old**   4
rich and **poor**   2
Democrat and **Republican**   2
black, white   2
Hispanic, Asian, Native-American   3
gay, straight   2
disabled and **not-disabled**   2
Americans who **sent** a **message** to the **world**   4
that we have **never** been **just** a **collection** of **individuals**
    or a **collection** of **red-states** and **blue-states**   7
we are and **always** will be the **United-States-**   2
    of-America

The two 6s are actually 5s, when you consider that (in line 1) *answer* is a repeat of *answer* in the preceding 'tonight is your answer', and that (in line 3) *hours* is used twice. In information terms, *three hours and four hours = three and four hours*. And the surprising 7 is actually 6, with *collection* being used twice – or even 5, if you reflect on how little is actually being added semantically by the intensifying word *just*.

Obama's opening sentence contains three instances of *still* plus verb. That's not by chance. It's another instance of careful planning. In fact, if any number is magical, in the context of eloquence, it's the number three. And also – noting the parallelism that binds the chunks in the third paragraph – the number two.

Shakespeare was there first

Generations of schoolchildren have been told that, if they know nothing else about Shakespeare, they should know that he wrote in iambic pentameters. They aren't usually told why.

The answer is not that it was the literary fashion of the day. That's true, but it begs the question. *Why* was it the fashion of the day? What is it about the iambic pentameter that made it so appealing to the dramatists of the time?

'The magical number five' is the answer. An iambic pentameter is a line of five 'te-tum' beats, each one of which can be the focus of a unit of information (shown here with a slash):

How sweet / the moonlight / sleeps / upon / this bank
I come / to bury / Caesar / not to / praise him.

It became the heartbeat of much succeeding English poetry:

> The curfew / tolls / the knell / of parting / day
>
> > (Thomas Gray)
>
> And all / that mighty / heart / is lying / still
>
> > (William Wordsworth)

Only a small proportion of the verse lines in Shakespeare are totally regular metrically, but the vast majority are 'of a length', and the chunks of information they convey are typically four or five. This makes them easy to process as a listener – and easy to remember if you're an actor. In Elizabethan theatre, actors had to present a fresh play every day, with a very short time to learn their lines. The five-unit line would have been the most facilitating of measures.

11

How do they do it? The rule of three

If there's one thing that seems to promote eloquent language more than anything else I describe in this book, that is found repeatedly in the speech of any orator I've ever listened to, that appears in every language I've ever studied, it's the 'rule of three'.

Eloquence is infectious. You notice a clever trick in an eloquent speech and think to yourself, 'I could do that'. So you try it out. And if it works, you keep it in your repertoire. One of the best bits of advice if you're an inexperienced speaker is to listen to as many speeches as possible, and cherry-pick the successful strategies that you think will best suit your own personal style.

The rule of three is one of the oldest tricks in the eloquence business. All public speakers know that they can get a round of applause if they use a triple with structural parallelism:

I was with you yesterday!
I am with you today!
And I will be with you tomorrow! [Cheers]

You have to put it across effectively, of course, with a crescendo peaking on the third item. It would be a curiously bathetic effect if you started with maximum loudness on the first item and ended with a pianissimo on the third.

What you must never do, of course, is overdo it. Imagine a speaker who has just produced a triple like that. If he went on to immediately produce another one, the effect would begin to pall.

> I said this in Brussels!
> I said it in New York!
> And I am saying it now in London! [??Cheers]

If a rhetorical trick is used twice in quick succession, listeners begin to notice it, and that's the worst thing that can happen to a speaker. When the style gets in front of the message it becomes a distraction instead of a reinforcement. It's the same with any art form: seeing the brush strokes rather than the painting, or hearing the virtuoso playing rather than the concerto. The French essayist Michel de Montaigne makes the point: 'Shame on all eloquence which leaves us with a taste for itself not for its substance.'[13]

The strategy operates regardless of gender, age, class, or occupation:

> We now know that it is not government, but free enterprise, which is capable of creating wealth, providing jobs and raising living standards.
> > (Margaret Thatcher, 12 December 1990)
> Talk to your friends, your family, your neighbours.
> > (Hillary Clinton, 13 June 2015)
> ... a time defined by selfishness and greed, inculcated cruelty and institutionalized self-centredness ...
> > (Russell Brand, 28 July 2015)
> ... they should be more clear with us about who the military is fighting for, who our tax dollars are supporting and,

ultimately, how much does the prime rib cost?

(Lady Gaga, 20 September 2010)

And a powerful double triple from Aung Sang Suu Kyi:

> It is not enough merely to call for freedom, democracy and human rights. There has to be a united determination to persevere in the struggle, to make sacrifices in the name of enduring truths, to resist the corrupting influences of desire, ill will, ignorance and fear.[14]

If we explore their entire speeches, we find triples popping up all over the place, but not in such a way that they draw attention to themselves. That's the clever bit: to hide the virtuosity.

How is it done? By varying the way in which triples are used. It's not just clauses that can be grouped in threes. It could be phrases, single words, or whole paragraphs. Obama uses each of these in his next three paragraphs. Here they are in full, with the triples in bold and main pauses marked by dashes (and including any hesitancies, such as 'th' below):

> **It's - the answer** told by lines that stretched around schools and churches -- in numbers this nation has never seen -- by people who waited three hours and four hours -- many for the first time in their lives -- because they believed that this time - must be different -- that their voices - could be that difference.
>
> **It's the answer** spoken by young and old -- rich and poor -- Democrat and Republican -- black, white -- Hispanic, Asian, Native American, gay, straight – disabled and not disabled - Americans who sent a message to the world - that we have never been - just a collection of individuals or a collection of red states and blue states - we are and always will be the United States of America.

> **It's the answer** - th that led those - who've been told for
> so long - by so many to be **cynical - and fearful - and
> doubtful** about what we can achieve - to put their hands on
> the arc of history -- and bend it once more toward - the
> hope of a better day. - It's been a long time coming - but
> tonight - because of what we did **on this day - in this elec-
> tion - at this defining moment** - change has come to
> America.

Triples continue throughout the rest of the speech, as we'll see,
but at intervals, so that they don't become intrusive.

What tricks are used to fill the spaces between the triples?
A different stylistic technique is needed, to provide variety
and maintain pace, and the most common is the 'magical
number two' – the use of pairs, and pairs within pairs. Here's the
second paragraph again, but this time with the pairs in square
brackets:

> It's - the answer told [by lines that stretched around
> [schools and churches] -- in numbers this nation has never
> seen] -- [by people who waited [three hours and four
> hours] -- many for the first time in their lives] -- because
> they believed [that this time - must be different -- that
> their voices - could be that difference].

The 'by lines' and 'by people' contrast is a pair – but each contains
another pair. Note how, strictly speaking, the pairing is unnecessary. He could have said simply:

> lines that stretched around buildings ... by people who
> waited hours ...

but the pairing is semantically more concrete and rhythmically
more effective. A triad would have been unwise here, for the

underlying meaning is actually rather banal, and to keep it going would be to produce a feeling of padding:

> by people who waited three hours and four hours and five hours . . .

Speakers who haven't really got anything to say do this a lot. The speech fills the time, but listeners go away wondering what they got out of it.

Pairs, as with triples, have to vary if they're not to become boring. The main pairings in the second paragraph are quite complex – whole clauses. What Obama does in his third para-graph is, to my mind, the most daring piece in the whole speech: a list almost entirely consisting of pairs:

> It's the answer spoken by [young and old] -- [rich and poor] -- [Democrat and Republican] -- [black, white] - Hispanic, Asian, Native American [gay, straight] - [disabled and not disabled] - Americans who sent a message to the world - that we have never been - just [a collection of individuals] or [a collection of [red states] and [blue states]] - we [are and always will be] the United States of America.

Beware lists, especially lists of people! They're dangerous things, because they prompt listeners to notice who might have been left out – although that day I don't think anyone was counting. This was a hugely effective listing, which generated sporadic applause throughout.

You'll have noticed that the pairs aren't all the same. Some pairs are linked by *and*, and some aren't. The 'collection' pairing is linked by *or*. Why? Just as triads have to vary to avoid monotony, so do pairs. It could become a boring list otherwise. But there's a subtle semantic issue also. The omission of *and* reduces the force of the contrast and allows the suggestion that the list can be extended. Unlike *young and old* and the others, the list of ethnic groups is open-ended. It implies that there are other groups apart from the ones mentioned, and this suggestion is reinforced by an uncoordinated triple (*Hispanic, Asian, Native American* . . .). Notice how this effect would be lost if *and* were added: *Hispanic, Asian, and Native American.* Running straight on to *gay, straight* without a pause also helps to avoid giving the impression that the list is complete.

As I mentioned in Chapter 6, eloquence is two-sided: you have to know what to say and also what not to say. It's the same for rhetorical structures such as pairs and triples. You have to know when to use them and when not to use them. Obama's next section is a good illustration – a series of paragraphs of acknowledgments and thanks. It needs to be quoted at length, as it's a complete change in content, tone, and pace, and displays a different kind of eloquence:

A little bit earlier this evening - I I received - an extraordinarily gracious call from - Senator McCain. --- Senator McCain fought long and hard in this campaign, -- and he's - fought even longer and harder - for the country that he loves. -- He has endured sacrifices for America - that most of us cannot begin to imagine. -- We are better off for the service rendered by this brave and selfless - leader. -- I congratulate him -- I congratulate Governor Palin - for all that they've achieved, - and I look forward to working with them - to renew this nation's promise in the months ahead. ---

I want to thank - my partner in this journey, -- a man who campaigned from his heart - and spoke for the men and women he grew up with on the streets of Scranton, - and rode with on the train home to Delaware, - the vice president-elect of the United States, Joe Biden. ---

And I would not be standing here - tonight without - the unyielding support - of my best friend - for the last sixteen years, - the rock of our family, - the love of my life, - the nation's next First Lady, - Michelle Obama. ---

Sasha and Malia, -- I love you both more than you can imagine, - and you have earned the new puppy that's coming with us to the White House. ---

And while - she's no longer with us, -- I know my grandmother's watching, -- along with the family that made me who I am. -- I miss them tonight -- I know that - my debt to them is beyond measure. --

To my sister Maya, - my sister Auma, - all my other brothers and sisters, - thank you so much for all the support that you've given to me. - I am grateful to them. ---

To my campaign manager, - David Plouffe, - the unsung hero of this campaign who built the best - the best political campaign I think in the history of the United States of America --- to my - chief strategist, David Axelrod -- who has been -- a partner with me every step of the way - to the best campaign team ever assembled in the history of politics - you made this happen, - and I am forever grateful - for what you've sacrificed to get it done.

But above all, -- I will never forget who this victory truly belongs to. -- It belongs to you. - It belongs to you.

It's a highly personal sequence (pathos) and this kind of sincerity needs to be expressed in a more loosely structured language. No climactic rhetoric wanted here. Sentences are shorter, the vocabulary is more private and down-to-earth, and the only hint of elaborate structuring is a single triple in honour of his wife: *the rock of our family, the love of my life, the nation's next First Lady*. The contrast with the rousing first section is striking. People cheered, but they were cheers of affirmation or sympathy rather than of triumph.

When you're analysing a speech like this, it's always interesting to pretend to be the speechwriter, and try out alternatives.

For instance, take the last sentence of the paragraph focusing on Obama's defeated election opponents:

> I congratulate him [McCain], -- I congratulate Governor Palin - for all that they've achieved, - and I look forward to working with them - to renew this nation's promise in the months ahead.

What would happen if we added in a triple here?

> I congratulate him, - I applaud him, - I salute him . . .

or here?

> . . . for all that they've achieved, - for all that they're achieving, - for all that they will achieve . . .

The effect is immediately one of insincerity. Deep down, everyone knows, especially after a heated campaign, that praise of an opponent is conventional politeness, even if it is genuinely meant. You don't expend the rhetorical energy of a triple on a conventional statement. Triples here would sound hollow or, worse, sarcastic.

By contrast, what would happen if we took the one piece of elaborate rhetoric in this sequence and cut that down to size?

> And I would not be standing here tonight without the unyielding support of my best friend for the last sixteen years, the nation's next First Lady, Michelle Obama.

Compared with the original, I feel somewhat underwhelmed. And – imagining myself in Obama's position – a less-than-glowing tribute could result in a cool homecoming. 'Am I only your best friend?'

Three centuries of triples

There's nothing new about the use of eloquent triples. Here is an example from a century ago, from the middle of Emmeline Pankhurst's 'Freedom or death' speech delivered in Hartford, Connecticut, on 13 November 1913:

> When they put us in prison at first, simply for taking petitions, we submitted; *we allowed them to dress us in prison clothes; we allowed them to put us in solitary confinement; we allowed them to put us amongst the most degraded of criminals;* we learned of some of the appalling evils of our so-called civilization that we could not have learned in any other way. It was valuable experience, and we were glad to get it.

A double triple in Thomas Babington Macaulay's speech to the House of Commons on the Reform Bill, 2 March 1831:

I will not, sir, at present express any opinion as to the details of the Bill; but having during the last twenty-four hours given the most diligent consideration to its general principles, I have no hesitation in pronouncing it a *wise, noble, and comprehensive measure*, skilfully framed *for the healing of great distempers, for the securing at once of the public liberties and of the public repose, and for the reconciling and knitting together of all the orders of the State.*

From an essay by Thomas Paine in *The American Crisis* (1776), ordered by General Washington to be read to the troops at Valley Forge a year later:

Say not that thousands are gone, turn out your tens of thousands; throw not the burden of the day upon Providence, but 'show your faith by your works', that God may bless you. It matters not where you live, or what rank of life you hold, the evil or the blessing will reach you all. *The far and the near, the home counties and the back, the rich and the poor*, will suffer or rejoice alike.

12

How do they do it? Weight control

Even good speakers and speechwriters can get triples wrong. This one of Obama's was slightly flawed:

> ... new energy to harness, new jobs to be created, new schools to build ...   4 + 5 + 4 [number of words]

It would have been more effective to avoid the passive construction and maintain the parallel, producing a more dynamic impact:

> ... new energy to harness, new jobs to create, new schools to build ...   4 + 4 + 4

The passive construction always distances the speaker from the action. It's a useful construction if you want to say that something happened but don't want to say who did it. That's why newspaper billboards, wanting to evoke curiosity (and thus get someone to buy the paper), tend to say things like:

TWENTY KILLED

and not:

TWENTY KILLED BY UNEXPECTED TORNADO

which removes the curiosity from a potential purchaser. But it can be a dangerous strategy in a political speech. To say that 'new jobs are to be created' similarly leaves the question open: 'by whom?' A political opponent could pick on that and make something of it. It was an odd choice for Obama, seeing that the other two verbs in the string are active and dynamic.

When the agent (the *by* phrase) is expressed, there is another effect: it places the interesting part of the sentence at the end. The weightier bit of meaning, in *Twenty killed by unexpected tornado*, comes after the verb. This actually conforms to the normal way English clauses work in everyday conversation. The bulk of the clause (the 'weight') appears after the verb rather than before it. Which of these two sentences is more natural, easier to process?

It was nice of John and Mary to come and visit me the other day.

For John and Mary to come and visit me the other day was nice.

It's a no-brainer. Everyone would say the first was the more natural style. And this principle permeates English grammar. Most everyday sentences have a grammatical subject that is just one or two words – usually a pronoun (*I* . . ., *We* . . ., *It* . . .) or a short noun phrase (*My friend said* . . ., *The answer is* . . .). When it comes to easy comprehension, respecting end-weight is crucial.

We notice cases when the speaker fails to respect it. If a speaker starts off with a lengthy grammatical subject and keeps us waiting for the verb, there comes a point when we begin to lose track and start thinking 'get on with it' or 'what's it all about?' This sort of thing:

My party, which has served you faithfully for the past five years, and which has fulfilled every one of its election promises, and which is prepared now to serve you again if you put your trust in us, and if . . .

'Where's the verb?' I shriek silently. Eventually it comes – if the speaker doesn't lose track. (It's not unusual to hear such sentences where the verb never surfaces.) But we have to remember how the sentence started in order to make sense of the ending:

. . . and if you place your cross in the right box on polling day, I proudly represent tonight.

Sometimes the speaker senses that the subject has been lost sight of, and adds a reminder:

. . . and if you place your cross in the right box on polling day, *that party* I proudly represent tonight.

But even with a recap, the weight of a long grammatical subject can break listeners' attention tolerance. By contrast, putting the verb first immediately makes us more comfortable with the sequence of clauses that follow, because we know where the speaker is going:

I proudly represent tonight the party which has served you faithfully . . .

We feel that the speaker is getting down to business.

Obama's speech is an example of someone doing exactly that. Here's the beginning of all his sentences in one of his paragraphs, with the verb in bold (and ignoring the pauses). Simply note where the length of each clause lies.

I **was** never the likeliest candidate for this office.

We **didn't start** with much money or many endorsements.

Our campaign **was not hatched** in the halls of Washington.

It **began** in the backyards of Des Moines and the living rooms of Concord and the front porches of Charleston.

It **was built** by working men and women who dug into what little savings they had ...

It **grew** strength from the young people who rejected the myth of their generation's apathy ...

It **drew** strength from the not-so-young people who braved the bitter cold ...

This **is** your victory.

Just one or two words before the verb. That's not only conversationally normal, it's excellent public speaking practice too, because it ties in closely with the way speakers use the rhythm and melody of speech, where the point of greatest prominence comes after the verb. I'll talk more about that later.

The vast majority of triples make use of the principle of end-weight, as in these Obama examples. The numbers show an increase in word length, especially in the last item:

... two wars, a planet in peril, the worst financial crisis in a century   2 + 4 + 7

... how they'll make the mortgage or pay their doctors' bills or save enough for their child's college education
3 + 4 + 7

... block by block, brick by brick, calloused hand by calloused hand   3 + 3 + 5

Other instances can be seen in the Thatcher, Brand, Gaga, and Suu Kyi quotations in Chapter 11, and those from Pankhurst and Macaulay in the related Interlude. Note that the end-weight principle can apply to single words too, with the number of syllables in the word increasing, as in the Macaulay sentence:

> I have no hesitation in pronouncing it a *wise, noble, and comprehensive measure.*   1 + 2 + 4

Some triples don't make use of end-weight. They are perfect parallels, using the same grammatical construction and containing exactly the same number of words, as in the examples from Hillary Clinton and Thomas Paine. Obama uses them too:

> ...Americans who volunteered and organized and proved ...   1 + 1 + 1
> ...partisanship and pettiness and immaturity ...
>   1 + 1 + 1
> ...a government of the people, by the people, and for the people ...   3 + 3 + 3

Their succinctness, of course, makes them extremely memorable, and prime candidates for inclusion in books of quotations.

I think everyone has an instinct for the power of an end-weighted triple. At a wedding reception, I remember this concluding sentence from a best man who said he had never spoken in public before:

> I hope you two have a fantastic honeymoon, a long and happy marriage, and have lots and lots of wonderful children that grow up to be as handsome as me.

I don't recall anything else from the speech. And it may have been my imagination, but I felt other potential best men in the room were making a mental note: 'I can use that.' Triples do tend to stay with you.

Magical foursomes

For parallel structures to work, the sequence must be capable of being retained in working memory, otherwise the effect will be lost. This is easy with pairs and triples, and it's just about possible with fours, as long as the elements aren't too long.

Here is Winston Churchill:

> I have nothing to offer but blood, toil, tears and sweat.
> In war: resolution. In defeat: defiance. In victory: magna-nimity. In peace: goodwill.

More than four, and the sequence would very likely lose its unity, and be perceived as a list.

13

How do they do it? Order, order

Another important feature of successful eloquence (or successful writing) is the role played in comprehension by what is called 'order of mention'. It's a critical feature of good storytelling and clear instructions. And if it's not there, you notice it.

Imagine you've just bought a self-build kit from a store, and the instructions go like this (as they often do):

Step 1: Find strut A and strut B, and screw the green ends together using one of the screws P.

Step 2: Find strut C and strut D, and screw the green ends together using one of the screws P.

Step 3: Join struts A/B and C/D at the red end using one of the screws P.

Important: always ensure that, before you join any struts together, you use a washer T.

At this point, having carefully joined the four struts together, you howl, as you have failed to use washers T. You unscrew, grumbling, and start all over again.

The manufacturer has let you down by not respecting order of mention. It's a principle that can be easily stated: say first what must be done first; say second what must be done second; and so on. In these instructions, they have said fourth what should have been said first. They have broken order of mention.

It's the same with storytelling. Most stories begin at the beginning of an event and move steadily through to the end. We learn this before we even get to school:

> Once upon a time there was a little girl who lived in a house at the edge of a forest. One day she left home to go to school. On the way she saw a beautiful pink flower. She decided to call it Eleanor . . .

English of course allows us to break order of mention if we want to, but it's a risky strategy, as it makes the listener/reader think harder. Here are some examples where the first thing that's said is the second thing that has to be done or that happened:

> Before you take the pills, read the accompanying leaflet.

> In 1666 there was a Great Fire in London. The year before, there had been a Great Plague.

And in this example, the second thing that's said is the first thing that has to be done:

> You should read the instructions after you've read the introduction.

Words like *before* and *after* switch order of mention. They make sentences a little bit more difficult to process. Young children don't learn to handle them until after they've learned the basic storytelling technique, which is 'this happened, and then this happened, and then this happened . . .'. We would never expect a children's story to begin like this:

> Once upon a time, before a little girl who lived in a house at the edge of a forest saw a beautiful pink flower, and decided to call it Eleanor, she left home to go to school.

It's the same content, and actually uses fewer words, but it's hopeless writing. And it would be hopeless speaking, if such a back-to-front style were used in the storytelling part of a speech.

By 'story', of course, I mean any narrative that presents a sequence of events. It is far more than fiction, and includes lecturing expositions, life summaries (as in a prize-giving or a best-man's speech), and the marshalling of historical facts, as in this famous example – the statement made from the dock by Nelson Mandela at the opening of his trial on charges of sabotage (20 April 1964). He strictly follows order of mention, as shown by the critical connecting words (in bold):

> The African National Congress was formed **in 1912** to defend the rights of the African people which had been seriously curtailed by the South Africa Act, and which were then being threatened by the Native Land Act. **For thirty-seven years** – that is **until 1949** – it adhered strictly to a constitutional struggle. It put forward demands and resolutions; it sent delegations to the Government in the belief that African grievances could be settled through peaceful discussion and that Africans could advance gradually to full political rights. But white governments remained unmoved, and the rights of Africans became less instead of becoming greater. In the words of my leader, Chief Lutuli, who became President of the ANC **in 1952**, and who was **later** awarded the Nobel Peace Prize . . .

And so it continues. This is an eminently sensible strategy in a difficult speech situation where a complex story has to be told. We can sense the extra load on comprehension if, for example, the last sentence had been:

> In the words of my leader, Chief Lutuli, who was awarded the Nobel Peace Prize in 1961, and who had become President of the ANC in 1952 . . .

This isn't just my impression. A great deal of research has been carried out into the way people respond to such changes. People are presented with a sentence structured in different ways and told to perform the actions:

> A Press the green button and then press the red button.
> B Before you press the green button, press the red button.
> C Press the green button, after you press the red button.

They respond most quickly to A, less quickly to B, and least quickly to C. While such differences might be trivial in an easy-to-follow story, such as when telling a joke, they can become all-important when taking an audience through an intricate narrative, such as an explanation of a scientific experiment.

The sentence about the Great Fire and Plague was actually taken from a history book aimed at children aged around ten. Here's the whole paragraph:

> In 1666 there was a Great Fire in London. The year before, there had been a Great Plague. The fire put paid to the plague.

I was in a classroom observing a teacher asking questions about the book to check on comprehension. When she got to this point, I suggested she read the paragraph aloud, then ask the class the following question and get them to write down the answer: 'Which came first, the fire or the plague?' She thought it was a rather pointless exercise, but she did it, and was amazed at the results. Half the class thought the fire happened first.

That is what can happen when order of mention is broken. Comprehension is lost. And the misunderstanding may have consequences for later learning if the mistake isn't noticed and corrected. In this case, the reversal was signalled by the phrase *the year before*. If the children don't notice that, they'll assume that the first thing that was said was the first thing that happened. And evidently quite a few of them fell into the trap.

It would have been easier for them if the author had written:

In 1665 there was a Great Plague in London. The next year, there was a Great Fire. The fire put paid to the plague.

But writers like to break order of mention from time to time, because it adds variety, and avoids a style of 'this happened, then this happened', which can become boring. There's nothing wrong with that, as long as they remember that they're making their readers work that little bit harder to access the meaning. Speakers need to remember the same thing.

The great Q

The importance of good sequencing in speech is referred to several times in the writing of Marcus Fabius Quintilianus (see Chapter 3). For example, we read:

> Just as the current of rivers is more forcible in a descending channel, which offers no obstruction to their course, than amidst rocks that oppose their broken and struggling waters, so language that is properly connected and flows on with a full flood is preferable to that which is rugged and fragmentary.[15]

Later in the chapter, he acknowledges both normal order-of-mention and the need sometimes to depart from it:

It is far too exacting a proof to always place first that which is ordered first in time, not that this order is not frequently preferred, but because that which precedes is often of greater importance and should consequently be placed after what is of less.

For the humanist writers of the sixteenth century, much concerned with the nature of rhetoric, there was none greater than Quintilian. Erasmus went so far as to precede his remarks on the art of instruction by a disclaimer: 'It seems a mere impertinence in me to handle afresh a subject which has been made so conspicuously his own by the great Quintilian.'[16]

14

How do they do it? Variation

One of the things actors know is that, in a long speech, they have to leave themselves somewhere else to go. If you put all your energy into the opening lines of a soliloquy, you'll find it trailing away into nothing before the end. Rather, start low and steadily build up. Or, divide your speech into sections and introduce peaks and troughs. Or, divide it into sections and treat each section in a different way. Whether you're speaking at a rally or a wedding, the principle is the same.

Here's how Obama did it. The middle-game of his speech has several sections, each very different in content, and it's the switch of content that motivates a switch of style and renews the audience's motivation to listen. There's no recapitulation or anticipation. It's string-of-pearls speech-making (Interlude 9, p. 73). If I characterize each section by a single word or phrase, I imagine this wouldn't be far away from the writers' notes when they first began to plan the speech.

So, after the 'thanks' section described in Chapter 11, with its rhetorical lull, we get:

- a 'story of the campaign' section,
- a 'scale of the problem' section,

- a 'challenges to our nation' section,
- a 'new dawn' section.

And with renewed political messages comes renewed rhetorical structure. The triples return:

> I was never the likeliest candidate for this office. --- We didn't start - with much money or many endorsements. -- Our campaign was not - hatched in the halls of Washington; - **it began in the backyards of Des Moines - and the living rooms of Concord - and the front porches of Charleston**. -- It was built by working men and women who dug into what little savings they had to give **5 dollars - and 10 dollars - and 20 dollars** to the cause . . .

And the pattern continues, with triple after triple building up momentum.

The 'new dawn' section used two time-honoured speech-ending techniques. First there was a sequence of four rather than three:

> tonight we proved once more that the true strength of our nation comes not from the might of our arms or the scale of our wealth, but from the enduring power of our ideals: - democracy, - liberty, - opportunity - and unyielding hope. ---

That slows the pace down. End approaching. And then there was an appeal to the future:

> That's the true genius of America, -- that America can change. -- Our union can be perfected. -- And what we have already achieved gives us hope for what we can and must achieve tomorrow.

Definitely end approaching.

When I heard this speech for the first time, I thought that was it. But then there was an electrifying change. The end-game was still to come. And it took the form of a story. Obama had definitely left himself somewhere else to go.

I wasn't expecting a story at all in a victory speech. As I suggested in Chapter 8, stories are an invaluable way of starting a speech. They help break the ice. But there's no ice waiting to be broken in a victory speech. So there was no opening story. And by the time Obama had finished going through his string of pearls, I was expecting the speech to end. It didn't.

The concluding section was totally different in style from everything that had gone before. In one sentence he moved from the general and abstract ('America can change') to the particular and concrete:

> This election had many firsts - and many stories that will be told for generations. But - one that's on my mind tonight's about a woman - who cast her ballot in Atlanta. -- She is a lot like the millions of others who stood in line to make their voice heard in this election - except for one thing: - Ann Nixon Cooper is 106 years old.

It was a risky strategy. He had just produced fifteen hundred words of highly crafted rhetoric, with many vivid and emotive images – *from parliaments and palaces*, *America's beacon still burns as bright*, *the true genius of America*. The audience is being brought to the boil. To tell an intimate story now could have produced an anticlimax. But it didn't. Why?

Because the speechwriters had a trick up their sleeve. The Cooper story starts quietly:

> She was born just a generation past slavery . . .

but within a few words she is part of a new rhetorical build-up, first with a pair:

> ... a time when there were no cars on the road or planes in the sky ...

and then a stunning triple, with each element containing a pair:

> I think about all that she's seen throughout her century in America -- the heartache and the hope; - the struggle and the progress; - the times we were told that we can't, - and the people who pressed on with that American creed: Yes we can.

There's the trick that gets the speech out of any possible trouble. The audience has already shouted 'Yes we can', three times, at an earlier point, and they are expecting more. The catchphrase had been used throughout the campaign. The real climax of the speech is waiting to build on that.

But an audience has to be taught what to do by way of reaction. People won't intervene en masse in the middle of a story. They have to be invited. And Obama uses the rule of three to teach them. That first 'Yes we can' gets no noticeable response from the crowd. Nor does the second:

> At a time when women's voices were silenced and their hopes dismissed, - she lived to see them stand up and speak out and reach for the ballot. - Yes we can.

But after the third, the crowd knows it need wait no longer:

> When there was despair in the Dust Bowl and - depression across the land, - she saw a nation conquer fear itself with a

New Deal, - new jobs, - a new sense of common purpose.
- Yes we can.
        AUDIENCE: Yes we can!

Four more 'Yes we can' responses follow, the last one closing the speech. And each of the short paragraphs that separate the crowd's shouts begins with a triple, like this one:

America, - we have come so far. - We have seen so much.
- But there's so much more to do.

When these triples focus on events in Ann Nixon Cooper's life, they respect order of mention, as all good stories should. I've added the dates to make the point.

She was there for the buses in Montgomery, the hoses in Birmingham, a bridge in Selma . . . [1955, 1963, 1965]
        A man touched down on the moon, a wall came down in Berlin, a world was connected . . . [1969, 1989, 1991]

The final paragraph of the speech ends with a burst of triples, like a linguistic fireworks display. I'll lay it out as I did earlier:

This is our chance to answer that call.
        This is our moment.
        This is our time -

to put our people back to work and open doors of
        opportunity for our kids;
to restore prosperity and promote the cause of peace;
to reclaim the American dream and reaffirm that
        fundamental truth

        that out of many, we are one;
        that while we breathe, we hope;

and where we are met with cynicism and doubt and
    those who tell us
that we can't, we will respond with that timeless creed
    that sums up the spirit of a people: Yes we can.

The last big clause isn't as well structured as the others. There's a curious grammatical dislocation between *met with* and *those who*. But by this point nobody is caring about grammar. It's the vocabulary that counts, and with 'dream', Obama ends as he began. 'Dream' is a powerful word in American political rhetoric because of the way it was used by Martin Luther King in his famous 'I have a dream' speech on civil rights in 1963. King isn't mentioned by name in Obama's speech, but he's there in spirit, from the beginning to the end. Obama's opening words link dreams to questions. His closing words link dreams to answers. The speech is a Martin Luther King sandwich, and it went down very well indeed.

It has been called – by those who have no party axe to grind – one of the great political speeches of our time. It won't rank with the very best (without editing) because the 'thank-you' section particularizes and personalizes too much. Gratitude to campaign managers and the like has no permanent resonance. But if the role of style is to get your content across as effectively as possible, then Obama and his speechwriters proved themselves to be stylists second to none.

Great eloquence, however, can have a downside, especially in politics.

Going beyond the rules

Variation points towards another great principle of eloquence: rules are there to be broken. To my mind, Martin Luther King's 'I have a dream' speech (28 August 1963, reproduced as Appendix 2 on p. 228) is the perfect example of this. What was it in the speech that allowed it to be called by that name?

It is a speech full of parallelism. Almost half of its eighty-two sentences ring the changes on a common initiating phrase. Not for King the limitations of the 'rules' of pairs and triples. There is just one pair ('We refuse to believe . . .') and one triple ('Some of you have come . . .') in the whole speech. Soon after the opening words, we have a sequence of four sentences beginning with 'One hundred years later . . .'. And then there is another four, beginning with 'Now is the time . . .'. But these fours are very different from the Churchillian ones (Interlude 12,

p. 100) because of their length, with up to twenty words following the cue phrase. This in itself is a departure from what most speakers do. But they are a foretaste of what is to come.

The speech steadily increases the number of sentences that are put into a parallel relationship. In answer to the question 'When will you be satisfied?' King gives us six parallel answers, with just minor variations in the phrasing: 'We can never be satisfied . . .'. Another six follows: 'Go back to Mississippi, go back to Alabama . . .'. And then the extraordinary memorable eight:

I still have a dream. It is a dream deeply rooted in the American dream.

I have a dream that one day this nation will rise up and live out the true meaning of its creed: 'We hold these truths to be self-evident; that all men are created equal.'

I have a dream that one day on the red hills of Georgia the sons of former slaves and the sons of former slave owners will be able to sit down together at the table of brotherhood.

I have a dream that one day even the state of Mississippi, a state sweltering with the heat of injustice, sweltering with the heat of oppression, will be transformed into an oasis of freedom and justice.

I have a dream that my four little children will one day live in a nation where they will not be judged by the color of their skin but by the content of their character.

I have a dream today.

I have a dream that one day down in Alabama, with its vicious racists, with its governor having his lips dripping with the words of interposition and nullification, that one day right down in Alabama little black boys and black girls will be able to join hands with little white boys and white girls as sisters and brothers.

I have a dream today.

I have a dream that one day every valley shall be exalted, every hill and mountain shall be made low, the rough places will be made plain, and the crooked places will be made straight, and the glory of the Lord shall be revealed, and all flesh shall see it together.

This is our hope.

This is daring parallelism, which virtually guarantees its memorability as a title. Apart from the remarkable number of items in the sequence, we should note their length: two of the pieces are over fifty words each. You have to be a very confident speaker to control such complexity. King manages it by a subtle recapitulation in the first case ('one day right down in Alabama') and in the second by using biblical phrases that will be well known to most of his audience ('every valley shall be exalted . . .'). And he precedes and follows each by using brief sentences that give the listener (and perhaps also himself) a moment of relaxation to take them in.

The speech might well have ended after the 'dream' sequence. But this is another fine example of an orator who has left himself 'somewhere else to go'. For he caps it with a sequence of nine – not lengthy and structurally diverse, as with the 'dream' sentences, but short and punchy, with exactly parallel internal structure:

So let freedom ring from the prodigious hilltops of New Hampshire.

Let freedom ring from the mighty mountains of New York.

Let freedom ring from the heightening Alleghenies of Pennsylvania.

Let freedom ring from the snow-capped Rockies of Colorado.

Let freedom ring from the curvaceous slopes of California.

But not only that; let freedom ring from the Stone Mountain
   of Georgia.
Let freedom ring from Lookout Mountain of Tennessee.
Let freedom ring from every hill and molehill of Mississippi.
From every mountainside, let freedom ring.

It might have been called the 'let freedom ring' speech, as a consequence, and indeed some do refer to it in that way. But the 'dream' metaphor has overshadowed it. Either way, what was heard on that day was the potential of parallelism exploited to an exceptional degree.

How do they do it? Being natural

Fantastic political eloquence has its critics. If you are too eloquent, your opponents will accuse you of being facile, glib, only a wordsmith. 'It's time for action from the man of words' said a headline in the *Telegraph* (18 January 2009), and the writer went on: 'Barack Obama has a remarkable gift for oratory, but does it mask a fatal indecisiveness?' The criticism was repeatedly made throughout his administration. In January 2015, Carly Fiorina, an American business leader, later announced as a Republican presidential candidate, told Newsmax TV:

> He is a man of words. He has spent most of his life with words, speaking, and he seems to fail to understand that talking and acting are two different things. He seems to think that when he gives a speech, he has acted.

It's a widely used political ploy, to accuse your opponent of hiding behind words. Here's Lloyd Bentsen, accepting the Democratic nomination for vice president in 1988, being rude about Ronald Reagan's administration:

America has just passed through . . . an eight-year coma in which slogans were confused with solutions and rhetoric passed for reality.

And, in case anyone thinks this is a purely American strategy, here is Charles Dickens, aiming at British MPs:

Our honourable friend is triumphantly returned to serve in the next Parliament. He is the honourable member for Verbosity – the best represented place in England.[17]

The practice continues today, to the point of cliché:

Tory-led Government has been shown to be all talk and no action. (*Daily Express*, 20 December 2014)
Ed Miliband's Labour Party is all talk and no action. (*Socialist Worker*, 21 August 2013)
UKIP are all talk and no action. (*ConservativeHome*, 12 May 2014)

And so on. Any election campaign in any country will elicit such jibes.

The proverbial wisdom of generations takes up the theme. Never trust eloquent people. Don't believe what they say. Words won't get a job done.

Behind big words dwells a little soul. (Switzerland)
Where there is least heart there is most speech.
                              (Montenegro)
Many words, little sense. (Japan)
Talk does not cook rice. (China)
Fair words butter no parsnips. (Britain)

The danger is present for everyone who tries to speak well, not just politicians. It's possible for a wedding speech to sound insincere, or a lecture to sound thoughtless, if it's spoken in too smoothly loquacious a manner. It can also place a strain on the listener. As Blaise Pascal said, 'Continuous eloquence wearies.'[18]

So, if this is an ever-present danger, can it be avoided? Are there ways of stopping eloquence drawing attention to itself and tiring the listeners out? Yes there are. The trick is to make the speech sound more natural, more like the language we would use in an everyday conversation – but not exactly like it.

When we talk to each other in daily life, our language is spontaneous, unplanned, informal. It's not carefully crafted, as it would be in a formal speech or when reading a prepared text. We hesitate, repeat ourselves, leave sentences loosely connected and unfinished, avoid being absolutely precise, and add tiny remarks – they're often called 'fillers' – that tell our listener we're working out what to say or how to say it. Here's a tiny extract from a recording of a conversation that illustrates these points:

> So, we decided – well, I say we – Jane decided that we shouldn't go for a new car this year cos cos – well to be honest, things are a bit, you know, tight, and although the old car's um sort of creaky at least it does still – go, and gets us about . . .

Informal conversational style is characterized by these fillers (*well, to be honest, you know, sort of*), repetitions (*cos cos*), hesitations (*um*), pauses in unexpected places (*still – go*), and loosely connected sentences (*so . . . and . . . and . . .*). Some people try not to use them, believing them to be a sign of unclear speech, but in fact everyone speaks like this to some extent. Most of the time we don't even realize we're doing it. Fillers have been called the oil that makes a conversation run smoothly.

We describe speakers as non-fluent if they overuse these features to the point where they become noticeable, begin to irritate, and interfere with communication. It becomes distracting when someone says *you know* or *I mean* or *like* in every sentence, or even several times in a sentence. And it really jars when we hear someone doing this in a situation where we expect fluency, such as on the radio. I recall someone being interviewed who was asked a straight question and who began his reply with something like:

> well, yes, thank you, erm, that's that's a, you know, a really really interesting question, because erm, you see I mean . . .

and he continued in that vein, with islands of content occasionally appearing above the surface of the waffle. This is as far away from eloquence as you could possibly get.

It's possible to see these features in a more positive light if we note the way they can individually affect the meaning of what we say. Compare the following pairs of sentences, and you'll get a sense of what the *you know* filler can do, for example:

> I think you ought to leave.
> You know, I think you ought to leave.

(The *you know* softens the force of the statement. Without it, the sentence sounds abrupt, even aggressive.)

> I bought it in the shop on the corner
> I bought it in the shop – you know, the shop on the corner.

(The speaker thinks that *shop* will be clear, and then realizes it might not be. Here the *you know* acts as an alerting mechanism: what follows is the thing to pay attention to.)

> I've just seen John and his friend.
> I've just seen John and his, you know, friend.

(Now the *you know* is suggesting there's something special about the relationship.)

So when I say 'make the speech sound more natural', I don't mean making it sound like an everyday conversation, with all the features present. I mean introducing the occasional drop of informality in places where the crafted eloquence might otherwise feel overpowering.

Obama does this several times in his victory speech. Indeed, his very opening clause contains two instances of a colloquial pause. If spoken in a totally fluent way, we would expect to hear this, with just two pauses to highlight the feature of the sentence that is about to be used three times (see Chapter 10):

> If there is anyone out there - who still doubts - that America is a place where all things are possible ...

What we actually get is this:

> If there - is anyone out there -- who still doubts - that America is a place where - all things are possible ...

What are those other two pauses doing? Obama has either learned the speech largely by heart or he's reading it from the autocue in front of him. He has no need to hesitate, to break up the natural rhythm of the construction. But he does, twice. Why?

The pauses help to make you forget that he's working with a prepared text. They give the impression that he's spontaneously thinking of what to say. They help to hide the linguistic sophistication which, as I showed in Chapter 10, underlies the whole opening sequence.

You might think this is just chance. But he does it again at the beginning of the next paragraph, and the next (along with a tiny stammer):

it's - the answer told by lines that stretched around
schools and churches . . .
it's the answer - th that - led those - who've been told for
so long . . .

And it's especially noticeable in the passages where he needs to
show personal (as opposed to presidential) sincerity within the
eloquence. Here he is praising Senator McCain:

a little bit earlier this evening - I I received - an extraordinarily gracious call from - Senator McCain ---

We get a pause before the name. There isn't one chance in a
million that he's having trouble remembering the senator's
name, so the pause here can't be an indication of a mental
processing difficulty. Rather, it's hinting at emotion. We all
know what happens when we're trying to say something really
emotional: we pause and stammer a bit. There's a tiny stammer-
like effect here too, on the pronoun *I*. Good grief, these effects
lead us to think, he really means it.

The impression of spontaneity continues throughout this
part of the speech. There's no grammatical need for a pause
between an auxiliary verb and a main verb, or between adjectives
and a noun. (We would certainly never insert a punctuation
mark in such places in writing.) But we get both:

and he's - fought even longer and harder . . .
this brave and selfless - leader . . .

A little later, his wife is introduced:

I would not be standing here - tonight . . .

As is his grandmother:

and while - she's no longer with us . . .

And the family:

I know that - my debt to them is beyond measure . . .

None of these pauses are actually required by English grammar, but they are highly appropriate, suiting the mood of the moment, and conveying a degree of sincerity that words by themselves could never achieve. I've no idea whether they were consciously introduced or whether they were a natural and spontaneous expression of an emotion welling up on the spot. Only a recording of the speech rehearsals would resolve that.

Whatever the reason, the effect is the same. Judicious pauses, along with a cautious use of other features of everyday speech, can enhance eloquence by helping to hide its artifice and to introduce a linguistic empathy with the audience, who instinctively identify with them, because they recognize them from their own daily conversational experience. But the operative words are 'judicious' and 'cautious'.

Sounding, erm, eloquent

Radio stations can be very aware of the way umming and erring turns off listeners. When I was doing my *English Now* series for BBC Radio 4, back in the 1980s, I learned a new technique from the studio managers. They would take a tape –

[For those who have never known this pre-smartphone technology: *tapes* were long reels of thin plastic on which sound was magnetically recorded. They were played back on a *tape recorder*. You would edit the tape by placing the tape in a special holding device and use a razor blade to cut out the bits of speech you didn't want to keep. You'd then splice the pieces together with some sticky tape. It took ages.]

– and cut out any really intrusive hesitation noises. It made the speaker sound quite fluent!

I learned a new word, as a consequence. De-umming.

16

Sounding – natural

In *The Ghost*, the eighteenth-century satirist Charles Churchill describes his character Trifle launching into a speech, and getting into trouble after a few dozen lines:

> Here TRIFLE cough'd (for *Coughing* still
> Bears witness to the *Speaker*'s skill,
> A necessary piece of art,
> Of *Rhet'ric* an essential part,
> And *Adepts* in the Speaking trade
> Keep a *Cough* by them *ready made*,
> Which they successfully dispense
> When at a loss for *words* or *sense*).[19]

A cough. A very useful device if you want to gain some thinking time. So is a drink of water. These are natural behaviours. They're understandable, forgivable. They don't reflect on the speaker's eloquence – as long as they're not done too often, so that they become an intrusive mannerism or an obvious delaying tactic.

The same point applies to any use of informal conversational features. Their aim is to reduce the impression that an eloquent speech is contrived, and thus not sincere. But if they're used too much, they themselves become the focus of attention, and the effect is lost. This is why people become interested in the vocal conversational idiosyncrasies of politicians. If you support the politician, you see these quirks as showing an honest attempt to speak from the heart; if you don't, you see them as a pathetic attempt to hide a dismal political record.

In February 2015 there was a documentary on BBC Radio 4 called 'Read My Lips: Why Politicians Speak the Way They Do'. Jonathan Powell, the former chief of staff for Tony Blair, went through some of the famous political speeches of the twentieth century. The programme focused on the main tricks of eloquence that I've already described, such as the 'rule of three', and was illustrated with recordings of Asquith, Macmillan, Reagan, Wilson, Blair, and others. I was asked to listen to the recordings and make some comments. What struck me more than anything else was the oratorical shift in the use of conversational features from the time of Asquith to that of Blair. I heard none in the Asquith speech – presumably a reflection of the greater formality of discourse used in the days of early radio recording – but many in the speeches and interviews of recent times.

All the features heard in Obama's speech recur, as this short selection illustrates:

Macmillan: It's er quite an effort to try and put our minds
    back . . .
Reagan: There's a - coincidence today . . .
Blair: I feel the - I feel the . . .
Miliband: You know - the other day I was in the park . . .
Blair again: [It's] not a day for sound bites really . . .

As in the previous chapter, the way to discover what these features do to a speech is to see what happens if the same phrases or sentences are used without them. What happens, for example, if we omit the filler *really* from Blair's sentence?

[It's] not a day for sound bites really.
[It's] not a day for sound bites.

The sentence now sounds definite. No messing. And if Blair were then to use a sound bite later in the speech, it would be an open invitation to his opponents to accuse him of inconsistency. The use of *really* avoids that danger: it tells us that Blair doesn't want to make sound bites, but if he has to, well then all right …

The quotation from Ed Miliband is another instance of the uses of *you know* that I described in the previous chapter. Here the force is stylistic, adding an informal note. It's friendly and matey. Compare:

You know - the other day I was in the park …
The other day I was in the park …

It's the vocal equivalent of him putting his arm around you or sitting down in front of a roaring fire while he tells you what happened. All politicians use fillers like this in interviews when they want to elicit a sympathetic reaction to the point they're about to make. It wouldn't work with some interviewers – like Jeremy Paxman, the filler-ignorer.

There aren't many features that we can manipulate in this way, but it's useful to know what they are, if only to avoid over-using them. The most commont ones are the 'voiced hesitations', as phoneticians call them, popularly referred to as 'ers and ums'. 'Voiced' here contrasts with 'voiceless hesitations' – in other words, silence – that also interrupt the flow of speech. They're an important index of mental processing. They show you're thinking. Or, on the radio, they show you're still there. Silence, on the radio, is the disaster scenario.

Actually, silence can disrupt everyday conversation too. A conversation between two people only works when both participants are vocally active. While A is speaking, B is commenting, providing vocal feedback in the form of *mm*, *uh-huh*, *I see*, *wow*, *yeah*, and much more. This is essential feedback. If you try withholding it, remaining silent while someone is talking to you, the conversation will soon break down. The speaker will think you're bored, not listening, upset, or having a seizure.

The same point applies to the speaker. We don't expect people to stop in the middle of a sentence and remain silent while they think of what to say next. Imagine you're talking about something that happened at an event and you suddenly forget the name of the person the story is about.

... and then she went right up to ——

What do you do at that point? You're desperately trying to bring the name to mind, and it won't come. Your listener is looking at you. You can't just stay silent. You have to find a way of telling your listener that you're working on the problem. That's what a voiced hesitation does:

... and then she went right up to erm ...

And if, after that pause, you still can't bring the name to mind, you can then change tack with fillers or questions:

... and then she went right up to erm ... oh dear, what was his name, you know ...

A single use of *er* or *erm*, in a public speech, can be very effective. But it does depend on where you place it. A speaker should never use it before making a precise claim, for example. It then conveys uncertainty where listeners expect confidence. Lecturers or politicians will convey a better impression of 'being in control of the facts' if they use the first of these two sentences rather than the second:

> There will be a saving for everyone of 10.5 per cent.
> There will be a saving for everyone of - erm - 10.5 per cent.

Any of us, trying to make a point eloquently, will find the impact reduced by an unfortunately placed *erm*.

What you mustn't do, especially in public speech, is repeat the feature. Nobody worries about the occasional *erm* when speaking, especially if the occasion is an informal one. But when used frequently, or repetitively, or in unexpected places, *erm*s jump out at you and begin to irritate. If listeners can hear the fact that you're thinking, the speech is hardly going to be thought eloquent.

Irritation always comes when a bit of language is used too often, so that people begin to notice it. It distracts listeners, which is the last thing you want to do if you're trying to get a point across. And worse, it can make them want to throw something at you. Worse, because – in the case of politicians – the consequence is not simply to lose attention; it may lose votes.

A single *erm* might not even be noticed. But two *erm*s one after the other sound ponderous, and three or more sound positively idle-headed. Try repeating this sentence, which I once heard in a political debate:

> This was a matter for the - erm - erm - erm - minister to decide.

The speaker was beginning to sound like Big Ben.

It isn't just hesitant speech that causes this effect. Any word in the language, really, can become an irritant if it is really used too often in a sentence, really, or in a paragraph where really all one wants the speaker to do, really, is STOP USING THAT WORD. Really?

Excessive voiced hesitation carries all kinds of negative outcomes, which are usually internalized by the polite listener rather than made explicit. Impatience is one. 'Get on with it!' 'Spit it out.' Incompetence is another. 'Do your homework!' Lack of professionalism is another. You'd expect radio and television announcers to be *erm*-less, but the sad reality is the opposite. I recall a presenter on BBC News 24 – where they say who they are before reading the news headlines – even hesitate in the middle of saying his name. As it were: 'The News Headlines at midnight. I'm David er Crystal.' There may have been a good reason for it. Perhaps the presenter was momentarily distracted by something coming through in his earpiece. But the effect was to make the speech sound amateurish.

Voiced hesitation can also be a source of humour. I remember a sketch by American comedian Shelley Berman, when he played an airline pilot addressing his passengers: 'Good evening, ladies and gentlemen, this is your pilot, Captain Holbrook. I just want to welcome you all aboard Flight 714 non-stop to er ... errrr ...'[20] The audience hooted.

The thing about mannerisms is that we notice them in other people and fail to recognize them in ourselves. That's why it's an invaluable step towards eloquence to get someone else to listen to your speech in rehearsal, or – these days, because it's so easy to do – to record it and listen to it yourself. Listen out especially for the items that really irritate people if overused – fillers such as *you know*, *I mean*, and *like*. The experience will never be the same as when addressing a live audience; but rehearsal always helps.

I remember my BBC producer, Alan Wilding, doing this to me when I started to broadcast regularly back in the 1980s. Apparently I would drop my voice too much when I got to the end of a paragraph, so that the final words couldn't be clearly heard. It was a simple matter to correct, to lift the pitch that little bit extra, and give the closing words a tad more energy. But I would never have noticed the habit if he hadn't pointed it out.

It's unfortunately something that is still prevalent in broadcasting. We hear a really interesting piece of music, and the programme presenter says afterwards:

> That was the Such-and-such Orchestra, under their conductor So-and-So, in a performance of Symphony number 6 in A minor by [inaudible].

Or:

> That was the Symphony number 6 in A minor by Gustav Mahler, performed by the Such-and-such Orchestra, under their new conductor Anthony [inaudible].

The pitch of the voice is high and loud at the beginning of the sentence, but then a diminuendo sets in, with a lowering of pitch, so that by the end, the voice is inaudible. I've lost track of the number of times, in the car, my wife and I simultaneously howl: WHO?

You need to rehearse a speech beforehand in any case, to check on its length – at least until you become so experienced that you can control your timing instinctively. Or, if it's a prepared text, read it through aloud. If there are pictures to show, or a PowerPoint presentation to include, and what you want to say isn't already in the written text, practise the commentary you expect to make. It all helps to avoid the kind of disaster I described in Chapter 4, where the speaker failed to keep to time.

Speaking impressively, but naturally, is the goal of eloquence. And to achieve it, speakers need to master all the elements of the speaking voice, such as their pitch level, their loudness, and – above all – their speed. If there's one factor in delivery that affects listeners more than anything else, it's speech rate. If the speaker is too fast, the message can be unintelligible. If too slow, it can be sleep-inducing. If exactly the same tempo is used throughout, it can be boring.

But what does 'too fast' and 'too slow' mean, exactly? What are the norms for effective public speaking? People speak faster in everyday spontaneous conversation than they do when speaking in public. Just how much faster? How is a balance to be achieved? Understanding the way speed works when we speak is an important step towards achieving a natural kind of eloquence.

WPM

Ignoring the opening 'Hello Chicago', the two hesitations, and the crowd's repeated 'Yes we can', there are 2,040 words in Obama's speech. It lasts for sixteen minutes and thirty-five seconds. That looks as if he's speaking at 123 words a minute (WPM).

But that's a false measure, because he pauses a great deal (as the 462 dashes in the transcript show), and some of the pauses are quite long, especially when he waits to acknowledge the crowd's applause. In fact, on my rough stopwatch count, they add up to four minutes fifteen seconds. If we subtract that from his total speaking time, we find an actual rate of 165 WPM.

Is that normal? We need to do some counting.

17

Rates of exchange

Words per minute don't actually give a very precise indication of a speaker's rate, for the obvious reason that they are of different lengths. A speaker who uses lots of long words, such as *imagination*, *fundamental*, and *Afghanistan* is going to end up apparently speaking a lot more slowly than someone using lots of short words. It's simple maths. If I speak at the rate of one syllable per second, and each word is one syllable, I will speak sixty words in a minute (if I don't pause). If each word is four syllables, I will be able to speak – depending on how quickly I say the unstressed syllables – less than half that number.

Words are not a precise measure, for that reason. And also because it isn't obvious what counts as a word. The CNN transcript of Obama's speech says *vice president-elect*, or should it be *vice president elect or vice-president elect or vice-president-elect*? One, two, or three? And what about *not-so-young* and *221*. I counted *221* as one word in my Interlude 16; but if it were written *two hundred and twenty one* it would count as five.

So, when phoneticians measure speech rate, they generally count the syllables, not the words. A-syl-la-ble-is-a-u-nit-of-speech-where-there-is-a-per-ceiv-a-ble-pulse-or-beat. It's a far more accurate method. On that basis, Obama's inter-pausal rate is 167 syllables per minute – not very different from the word-based rate in his case, but that's because the vast majority of the words in his speech (92 per cent) are just one or two syllables in length. He has kept it simple. (It's a side issue for the present chapter, but it's worth noting that there are only thirty words that are four syllables in the whole speech, and only eleven that are longer – words like *immaturity* and *determination*. The vocabulary is well within the grasp of ordinary people – a point all speakers to a general audience should bear in mind.)

Normally, in everyday English conversation, people speak (between pauses) at a rate of five or six syllables per second. One syllable per second, as in my maths example, would be very slow indeed. In fact I've only ever heard it when speech therapists are teaching stammerers to use what they call 'slowed speech' – a technique that can help them control their stammer. Try speaking at one syllable per second and you'll see how slow that is. Look at your watch and – say – this – sen – tence – with – one – syl – la – ble – per – se – cond. Not even the slowest public speaker goes at that rate. Though I must admit I did once hear an after-dinner speaker, who had had far too much wine, come perilously close.

And before I move on, note the reference to 'English'. Languages operate at different syllable rates because they have different structures and rhythms. The number of syllables a Japanese or Spanish newsreader manages to cram into a minute is far greater than the English equivalent. In a study in the journal *Language*, a team of researchers found that in sponta-neous speech samples Japanese speakers spoke at a rate of 7.84 syllables per second, followed by Spanish (7.82), French (7.18), Italian (6.99), English (6.19), and German (5.97).[21] If everyday expectations are for faster speech, it's likely that in public-speaking situations the speech will be faster too. But even in one language there's a great deal of variation. Some accents of

English are much slower than others, as reflected in the stereo-types of English West Country rustic folk and drawling Texans.

How fast you speak isn't only a matter of personality. True, some people are fast speakers, and some are slow, just as they vary in the rate at which they do things and walk around. But a lot depends on where you live and the kind of job you do. Several research studies have shown that people in cities walk faster than people in the countryside, and that people in prosperous coun-tries walk faster than those in undeveloped countries. Unsurprisingly, they talk faster too. If time means money, then the more walking/talking you can get through in a day, the better. So the points about speech rate in this chapter should be inter-preted cautiously. Speaking at a lunchtime meeting in the City, with everyone looking at their watches, is likely to prompt a faster presentation than one at the same time in deepest Ruralshire.

Five or six syllables a second might sound fast, but it's a natural speed in calm, informal conversation with domestic subject matter. Time yourself saying a sentence of ten syllables out loud, such as 'Did you manage to catch the bus today?' Ten syllables. I just did it and it took me two seconds. Some people would say this more slowly, some more quickly. But the average is five sylla-bles a second. If you're having a heated argument, the average will go up to seven or eight. If you're expounding a complicated topic, it may go down to three or four. And if you're feeling especially meditative or tired, it may go lower than that.

The exchanges in everyday conversation are quite fast, there-fore. If we spoke for a full minute at the rate of five syllables a second we would produce 300 syllables. But we need to breathe. And our grammar makes us pause at various points, especially at full stops, as well as between chunks of information. Varying our pace is important too, as I'll describe shortly. So when people talk about '300 syllables a minute', what they mean is that the various passages being spoken would add up to 300 if they were strung together without any pauses and without any changes in pace. It's a convenient average which helps us compare different kinds of speaking.

So what happens when we speak in public? All the circumstances I've discussed so far – the size of the room, background noise, listeners' variable attention, the nature of the occasion, the level of content difficulty – will motivate a slower delivery. Obama was talking at an average rate of 167 syllables a minute – and that's a normal rate for a speech in such an environment. It may seem slow, but in a large arena the words reach the different parts of the venue at slightly different times. The lag can sometimes be heard in an echo of what the speaker has just said. You have to keep the speed down.

The danger is always one of speaking too fast, even in a small room and with a small audience. Every self-help book on public speaking emphasizes this. Fast speech can harm diction – that is, the clear articulation of individual words. Slower speech not only helps the listener process the words more comfortably, it helps the speaker's language processing too. There's extra time to think what to say next. There's more of an opportunity to draw attention to important words. There's more time to look around the audience. Pauses enable this as well, of course, but pausing too much can be a distraction, as we saw in the previous chapter. It's the overall pace of the delivery that counts for most. With an audience where English isn't the first language, it's good practice to start slowly before speeding up to your norm.

The principle applies even if you're reading from a text. Usually the task of reading aloud slows you down anyway, but if the text is one you've read several times before, you can unconsciously speed up and leave your listener behind. It's a common fault in announcements over a public-address system, especially in settings where the same message is spoken day after day. I'm sure I'm not the only one, waiting for a train, to have missed hearing my destination called because the announcer has gabbled the list of stations. Airports are generally better, and Toronto airport best of all (in my experience).

I was once asked to advise a ferry company on problems with their on-board announcements. They'd been receiving complaints from passengers that the messages weren't intelligible, and because the content was often about safety and security procedures, the company was worried. As some of the speakers had noticeable regional accents, the in-house view was that these were getting in the way of understanding. But it wasn't that at all. The problem was simply that the announcers were talking too quickly, without realizing it. Even the captains, in their welcome-on-board message, fell into the trap.

I spent an interesting week working with staff to get them to slow down – role-playing announcements at different speeds so that they became more aware of the contrasts, getting them to speak in unison, and so on. The human resources manager at the time told me she saw an immediate and dramatic improvement on board. For such an improvement to last, of course, regular periods of training are essential, especially in a company where there's a high rate of staff turnover and announcements are made by European Union immigrants with a faster rate of speech. If speech-training top-ups aren't made, the bad habits will return.

If you want to develop a feeling for speech rate, a useful exercise is to listen to the average rate of speech in a setting you know well, such as a familiar radio or television newsreader or sports commentator, and try imitating. There's quite a lot of variation, but studies of English newsreading show that most presenters speak slightly slower than conversational norms, at around five syllables per second. That usually comes out at anywhere between 150 and 200 words per minute, depending on the word lengths in the text. Newsreading has by definition a high informational content, and words tend to be longer than in everyday speech. Sports commentaries vary more because of their need to keep up with the action, which may be as different as the frenetic vocal volleying of tennis to the leisurely meanderings of snooker.

Sports commentaries are also linguistically interesting because they illustrate better than any other kind of public

speaking the importance of varying speech rate. When, in football, the ball is being passed backwards and forwards among the
players, the rate is slow, reflecting the pace of the game at that
point, and it speeds up as the possibility of a goal approaches.
We use the same techniques ourselves in everyday conversation,
though not usually so dramatically. And eloquent public speakers
play with rate all the time.

Whatever our normal speech rate is, we can do four things to
vary it, which I like to describe in musical terms:

- allegro: a sudden increase in pace;
- lento: a sudden decrease in pace;
- accelerando: a gradual increase in pace;
- rallentando: a gradual decrease in pace.

We don't introduce these variations randomly. Rather, they
reflect the content of what we're saying.

Take allegro. Why do people introduce sudden bursts of
speed into their speech? The reasons are many and various. It
might simply be that they think their speed of speaking is inap-
propriately slow, and in correcting this end up speaking more
quickly than they had intended. Or they realize they're running
out of time. But there are usually good semantic reasons for
allegro speech. Here are five. (I'll show the allegro passages in
italics, and any lento with underlining.)

- They want to make a parenthetical remark, which they
  don't want the audience to pay much attention to: 'The
  important issue – *and the previous speaker has made a
  similar point* – is this – <u>how many times</u> . . .'
- They think they're about to be interrupted, so they speed
  up to forestall it: '. . . and that's the critical issue which –
  [Interviewer: 'But don't you think –'] which I really want
  to [Interviewer: 'Hang on a minute –'] – *no let me finish*

because this is a really critical issue – <u>are we ready</u> for a sudden increase in ...'

- They realize they're saying, or have just said, something unpleasant or unpalatable, or something that might be taken in the wrong way, so they speed up to get over it as quickly as possible and present new material that will capture the attention of their listeners: '... now I know mothers can be very possessive about such things, *though I know Jane's mother doesn't fall into that category at all* because <u>just look at that cake</u> ...'

- They think of something more interesting that they want to say, so they speed up to get to the new topic as quickly as possible: '... that surely has to be the main factor – *though I mustn't forget to add, in view of what the chairman was saying earlier*, that <u>next week's meeting</u> ...'

- They want to avoid going into something, perhaps because they're unsure of their facts, so they speed up to get to the safer ground ahead: '... nobody wants to see such a thing – *though of course I know there are all kinds of qualifications that might be made here* but I think it's safe to say that the <u>really central issue</u> is ...'

In this last example, the allegro was followed by a rallentando on the 'I think it's safe to say', followed by a lento in which the 'really central issue' was emphasized. This is a very widely used feature in political discourse.

Speech tempo is the primary feature governing the overall intelligibility of public speaking, but it doesn't work alone. Along with pausing, it governs the rate at which our content reaches the ear and brain of the listener. If the right speed is chosen, listeners will follow comfortably. But just how comfortably depends on how the stretches of speech are melodically intoned.

Rattyspeak

It's difficult to show features like allegro and lento in normal writing, which I think is why their linguistic function tends to be underestimated.

We can hint at lento by capitalizing. If I had written 'the Really Central Issue' at the end of the previous chapter, the caps would suggest a slower and more emphatic articulation. And we can show the slowing down of a single syllable using hyphens or extra vowels: 'Re-a-lly', 'I'd faaar rather you didn't'.

But there's no conventional way of showing a speeding up, unlessIrunallthewordstogether or hyphenate-all-the-words. Writers tend to avoid this for obvious reasons, and prefer to say things like 'John muttered rapidly under his breath' and '"Yes," he said abruptly'. But Ratty from Kenneth Grahame's *The Wind in the Willows* is an exception, when Mole asks him what's inside a luncheon basket:

> 'There's cold chicken inside it,' replied the Rat briefly;
> 'coldtonguecoldhamcoldbeefpickledgherkinssalad-
> frenchrollscresssandwichespottedmeatgingerbeerlemon-
> adesodawater –'
>
> 'O stop, stop,' cried the Mole in ecstasies: 'This is too much!'[22]

It would be too much to take in if a sequence like this were produced in everyday conversation. Unlikely, you might think? Not so. I have heard just such a rapidly spoken series of food-stuffs presented to me by a New York sandwich vendor. I had asked for the contents slowly, choosing item by item, and partly following his prompts: ham, tomatoes, mayo, rye bread . . . some dozen options in all. As he gave it to me, he recapitulated the lot allegrissimo. I decoded the last words only: '. . . on rye'. Sandwich-selling eloquence at its best.

18

The melody lingers on

Intonation is the melody of a language. It's one of the first things we notice when we hear a foreign language or an unfamiliar accent – the pitch of the voice rising and falling. We talk of some accents sounding 'musical', or some languages sounding 'sing-song'. And we notice the unappealing sound of a monotonous voice – speaking at one pitch level without any variation.

Eloquent speakers, by contrast, make the most of intonation, just as actors do. And – recalling the point from Chapter 1 that eloquence is extra-ordinary – they do it by varying their pitch in ways that aren't usual in everyday conversation. Next time you're in a place where people meet, such as a cafe, listen to the pitch level of the conversations at other tables. It's low. People generally talk using the bottom third of their voice register. And if they're making a series of statements in a 'matter-of-fact' way, most of the tones go in the same direction. Count from one to five in a completely unemotional way – or the other way round, like the Houston count-down controllers do before lift-off – and you'll hear the routine use of a single tone. For most accents of English, that tone is falling in pitch. For some – such as many accents in Wales, Scotland, and Northern Ireland – the tone rises. Children playing hide-and-seek usually count keeping the tones level until they come to the last one: '... 98, 99, **100**, coming, ready or not!'

It takes something special – an emotion such as excitement, enthusiasm, surprise, irritation, or puzzlement – to stimulate higher levels of pitch. Public speaking is one of those special factors. The desire to persuade or express conviction requires more vocal energy, and this translates into greater variation in pitch and loudness. But it isn't just rhetoric that motivates this. We mustn't forget the aesthetic side of eloquence. If a voice sounds interesting, people are more prepared to listen and pay attention. And intonation is the main way in which speakers can add interest to their delivery.

It also plays a critical role in helping our brain to process what we hear. We saw this operating in Chapter 10, where it proved possible to remember much longer sequences of numbers (such as a phone number) by chunking the string into two parts: 3615 / 8294 /. It's the intonation that enables us to do this. The first four numbers are typically spoken with a rising or level tone on the last one; there's a brief pause, here shown by the forward slash; and the remaining four are spoken with a falling tone on the last one, followed by another pause. This is a very common speech pattern: a rising tone followed by a falling one. Listen to someone reading the football results on the radio in the UK. Everton 3 / Liverpool 3. The first team has a rising or level tone; the second team has a falling tone. It's the combination of the two that helps us remember what's been said.

In these examples, the rising or level tone tells us that the utterance has more information to come. It's the falling tone that tells us it's finished. The pauses, which may be very brief indeed, tell us that each tone is conveying a unit of content. And this is the pattern we see governing public speaking, especially in situations where the speaker wants to control audience response. Let's go back to one of Obama's paragraphs. How does the audience know when to applaud in a long string of points like this? It's by using rising or level tones (shown here with the words carrying those tones in bold) to signal that the list is continuing.

> it's the answer spoken by young and **old** / -- rich and **poor** / -- Democrat and **Republican** / -- **black** / **white** - **Hispanic** / **Asian** / Native **American** / **gay** / **straight** / - **disabled** / and **not** disabled / - Americans who sent a message to the **world** / - that we have never **been** / - just a collection of **individuals** / or a collection of **red** states / and **blue** states / - we **are** / and always **will** be / the United STATES of America ---

The strong falling tone on *States* shows he's done.

But you have to be careful, when using a list like this, as it can degenerate into sounding routine. Shopping lists are like this. What do you want to buy today?

> I need some **eggs** / **butter** / **bread** / **milk** / **cheese** . . .

It's an open-ended list. There are other things you haven't mentioned. You're not bothered about remembering them all. It's a boring shopping list, no more. Each item has a rising or level tone, and the rate is constant. No one item is more important than any other.

So, when naming a series of people, beware making them sound like a shopping list. Votes of thanks are like that. You have to thank five people. Here they are:

> I offer my sincere thanks to Jane Jones / Mike Williams / Fred Smith / Mary Morris / and Ann Parry / for all the work they've put into this event today /

If read with a rising or level tone on each surname, and a constant rate, it's like a shopping list, or a station announcer's list of railway stations. It gives the impression that you're just saying the names for form's sake. Sincere? It doesn't sound like it. Whereas, if you put a falling tone on each name, and separate them by a longer pause, it immediately gives them a personality.

In many churches it's customary at a certain point in the service to list those members of the congregation who are sick or who have died. It's a common experience to hear readers going through the names at a rate of knots. When I'm training church readers I make them say each name with a falling tone, followed by a pause. It gives the names an individuality, a presence. After all, if the aim of the exercise is to get the congregation to remember and/or pray for these people, then they need to be given a fragment of time in which to do so.

These units of intonation have a single job to do: they give prominence to the content they contain, separating it from the rest of what is said. So, if I wanted to remind Americans of 'the enduring power of their ideals', I could say them in a single unit, like this:

democracy liberty opportunity and unyielding hope /

in much the same way as I might say a phone number. That would be ineffective and maybe even demeaning – 'Not that boring old democracy liberty stuff again!' I immediately give each one more identity and interest if I say them as a sequence of separate units with rising tones, ending on a falling tone:

democracy / **liberty** / **opportunity** / and unyielding HOPE /

but it still sounds like a shopping list. To convey to the audience the power of these words, you have to say each of them with a falling tone followed by a serious pause:

DEMOCRACY / - LIBERTY / - OPPORTUNITY /
- and unyielding HOPE /

Which is what Obama did.

There's usually more than a single word in an intonation unit. In everyday speech, these units are typically five or six words in length. Even if you can't identify the pitch changes, you can certainly hear the rhythm in a story like this next one. In each unit, one of the words is more prominent than the others, and it's these that convey the main message – what the story is chiefly about:

> last **Sunday** / I was coming back by **train** / when there was a horrible screeching of **brakes** / and it suddenly **stopped** / – it was just outside **Crewe** / – I peered out of the **window** / and saw an engineer walking along the **track** / looking very **worried** / . . .

You could pull out the prominent words and they would give you the story skeleton:

> **Sunday** / **train** / **brakes** / **stopped** / **Crewe** / **window** / **track** / **worried** / . . .

They're usually the last words in the intonation units.

If you say the units in that way, with the emphasis on the last words, you're telling the story, certainly, but in a matter-of-fact way. It has no drama. To give it some, you need to look out for places where it's possible to bring the emphasis forward:

> a **horrible** screeching of brakes /
> looking **very** worried /

By emphasising *horrible* you show your own feelings about the event; by emphasizing *very* you show the man's. It becomes your personal story, rather than a newsreading narrative, and your audience becomes more involved.

Of course there has to be a good reason for bringing the emphasis forward in this way. There'd be no point, for example, in stressing *engineer*:

and saw an **engineer** walking along the track /

Who else did you expect to see? A ballet dancer? A horse? There's only a point in having intonation draw special attention to a word if there's a good reason. A contrast is always implied. The screeching was horrible as opposed to normal. The man was very worried as opposed to being mildly worried.

Eloquent speeches often move the emphasis about in this way. It's something that happens in all languages, and the classical orators always paid special attention to it. The motivation to do so comes naturally most of the time. We instinctively know which word should be the most prominent one. But occasionally, it's worth reflecting on which of the words in a sentence are the ones you really want to emphasize. Personally, I think that paragraph from Obama would have been more effective if, given the context, he had ended with the emphasis on UNITED States of America. But what do I know?

Good speakers don't overdo the intonation units. It would be perfectly possible for me to tell the train story like this:

when there was a **horrible** / **screeching** / of **brakes** /

That seems justified by the drama of the moment. The separate units give special attention to each word. Now all three are part of the emotion of your moment. But if you carried on like that, giving each bit of the sentence its own emphasis, the effect would quickly pall:

> I **peered** / out of the **window** / and **saw** / an **engineer** / **walking** / along the **track** /

Why give special emotional prominence to ordinary words? What is there about peering or seeing or walking that justifies it? You're making your listeners look for special significance where there is none. A speaker like Obama can get away with a long series of short intonation units because each unit contains some content that is emotionally appealing to the audience. It needs a highly charged speaking situation to make it effective. It simply wouldn't work in a context where there's no reason for such a build-up of emotional energy:

> I'd like to **thank** / the **members** / of the **Rotary** Club / of **Newtown** / for the **invitation** / to **speak** to them / **today** / about the **latest** / **housing** developments / in the **town** / . . .

I say again: the normal length of an intonation unit is half a dozen words. There needs to be a special reason to make them shorter.

Or longer. A long intonation unit, with a single rhythm and no pauses, is dangerous, because – as seen in Chapter 9 – you risk straining your listeners' comfortable attention span. You wouldn't have a problem in the Rotary Club sentence because the content is conventional. Listeners know what to expect, so they can handle a forty-two-syllable, rapidly spoken intonation unit:

> I'd like to thank the members of the Rotary Club of Newtown for the invitation to speak to them today about the latest housing developments in the town / . . .

But you wouldn't get away with it in a sentence where there are several bits of new or sensitive content:

I'd like to thank my new mother-in-law for her generous present to us both of a sports car and my best man for missing the home match today in order to be **here** /

Rather it ought to be something like (with possible audience reactions):

I'd like to thank my new **mother-in-law** / [cheers] - for her generous present to us **both** / [aww] - of a **sports car** / [wow] - and my best man for missing the home match today in order to be **here** / [laughs]

This is the domestic survival of the intonationally fittest.

And the prosodically fittest. Prosody is a term familiar in the literary world, where it's used to talk about the metre of a poem. In linguistics it has a broader definition, referring to the way we can change the meaning of an utterance by varying its pitch, loudness, rate, or rhythm. All four dimensions work together to produce the overall impact of eloquent speech. I've discussed rate and pitch. How do loudness and rhythm operate in public speaking?

Rounding a sentence well

'Playful – playful warbler,' said Mr. Pecksniff. It may be observed in connexion with his calling his daughter a 'warbler', that she was not at all vocal, but that Mr. Pecksniff was in the frequent habit of using any word that occurred to him as having a good sound, and rounding a sentence well, without much care for its meaning. And he did this so boldly, and in such an imposing manner, that he would sometimes stagger the wisest people with his eloquence, and make them gasp again.

His enemies asserted, by the way, that a strong trustfulness in sounds and forms was the master-key to Mr. Pecksniff's character.

(Charles Dickens, *Martin Chuzzlewit*, 1843–44, Chapter 2)

19

Build-ups, beats, and breaks

Loudness and rhythm go together, for what is rhythm but loudness with a beat? As with rate and pitch, they have a double function: they provide the norm for a speaker, and they can be manipulated to produce different effects.

I talked about loudness level in Chapter 5. Obviously, speakers need to be heard, and if they have a naturally quiet voice, amplification will help them avoid vocal strain. 'Speak up' is one of the worst reactions you can have when you're trying to be eloquent. Interestingly, there's no opposite equivalent: one never hears 'Speak down!' And yet an overloud presentation – usually because the speaker projects too strongly into a microphone – can be worse, because it can be painful, especially if you happen to be sitting in front of one of the loudspeaker cabinets. It's another of the pre-talk checks you need to make, especially if you know you have a naturally sonorous voice and the hall is not so large. Loud speakers don't always need loudspeakers.

Maintaining a comfortable level of loudness is a prerequisite, but that says nothing about eloquence. Loudness becomes eloquent only when it is varied. And, as with rate, we can talk about what is possible using musical terminology. There are six options, all defined with reference to the speaker's normal level:

- forte: a sudden increase in loudness;
- fortissimo: an even greater increase in loudness;
- piano: a sudden decrease in loudness;
- pianissimo: an even greater decrease in loudness;
- crescendo: a gradual increase in loudness;
- diminuendo: a gradual decrease in loudness.

The loudness increases are the ones we most often encounter in public speaking. They're virtually obligatory at the end of a strongly rhetorical passage, such as this one in Obama's speech, where there's a crescendo build-up over three clauses:

> I have never been more hopeful - than I am tonight that <u>we will get there</u> - <u>I promise you</u> - <u>we as a people will get there</u> ---

If the crescendo has worked, the speaker needs the pause. The loudness level has to be reset to the speaker's norm. And there needs to be a contrast soon after, otherwise the effect of increased loudness will be lost. As with intonation units, speakers must never overdo it. And so it's to be expected that in the next passage from Obama's speech we find a diminuendo:

> but I will always be honest with you about the challenges we face -- I will listen to you - especially when we disagree -

Quietness can convey an intimacy that is even stronger in its impact than its opposite. When a speaker wants to say something really personal, piano can be more effective than forte.

A crescendo is particularly common in a rhetorical sequence of three or four, but it has to be supported by the content. It works well when there's a list of emotive words or phrases, as in this build-up:

> the enduring power of our ideals - democracy - liberty - opportunity - and unyielding hope

Liberty was louder than *democracy*, *opportunity* louder than *liberty*, and *unyielding hope* loudest of all. Each element in this sequence is capable of bearing an unlimited amount of loudness, so that the gradual crescendo was effective. But if the three elements in a triple are equal in importance, then the loudness level needs to stay the same:

> it began in the backyards of Des Moines - and the living rooms of Concord - and the front porches of Charleston -

It would have been inappropriate to increase loudness here, making *Charleston* the crescendo peak, because the whole point is to suggest that the three places equally contributed to the campaign.

As with intonation, maintaining a consistent level is a feature of eloquence that applies to any speaking situation where there are lists, especially lists of people to be recognized or thanked. Loudness variation, whether increase or decrease, needs to be motivated. There has to be a very good reason if one of the names in a vote of thanks is spoken forte/fortissimo or piano/pianissimo, as it makes the name stand out. But in a speech as a whole there needs to be some sort of variation if the voice is to sound interesting. A constant loudness level, whether loud or soft, becomes boring.

As does a constant rhythm. Rhythm is our perception of regularity in speech. Every language has its own rhythm. French, for example, has a rat-a-tat-a-tat rhythm, with each syl-la-ble-giv-en-e-qual-pro-min-ence. Phoneticians call it 'syllable-timed rhythm'. In English, most speakers have a tum-te-tum-te-tum rhythm, where the stresses fall at roughly regular intervals in the stream of speech. Phoneticians call it 'stress-timed rhythm'. Not all English speakers use it. The English-speaking world gives us several examples of people who speak English in a syllable-timed way. Much of the English heard in the Caribbean or the Indian sub-continent is like that. And it's a dominant element in Caribbean-style rapping.

The important point to note is that stress-timed rhythm in everyday conversation is 'roughly regular'. We don't speak in perfectly formed iambic pentameters. There's a big difference between me saying:

It's time to go I think the taxi's here.

and:

The curfew tolls the knell of parting day.

Both utterances have a stress-timed rhythm, but the two utterances have different properties. The impact of the poetic line is greatest when the metre is respected. It forms part of a line-sequence where the next lines have the same rhythm, and it is the steady rhythmical parallelism that contributes to the elegiac effect:

The curfew tolls the knell of parting day.
The lowing herd wind slowly o'er the lea,
The ploughman homeward plods his weary way,
And leaves the world to darkness and to me.
         (Thomas Gray, 'Elegy Written in a Country Churchyard')

But there is no such predictability in the conversational utterance. Whatever the speaker says next need not have the same rhythmical structure as the taxi sentence. And there are various ways of saying that sentence which allow the rhythm to be broken up and lose its regular character, such as introducing a pause before or after *I think*, or a jocular tone of voice on *go*.

Everyday conversation is rhythmically erratic, and this carries over naturally into public speaking, so that the speech doesn't sound like a series of iambic pentameters. But this allows speakers to introduce a rhythmical contrast, and when it happens it contributes greatly to the impression of eloquence. There are two options:

- rhythmic: more rhythmical than normal,
- arrhythmic: less rhythmical than normal.

Both variations can add extra meaning to a message.

To make a sentence more rhythmical, the stressed syllables are made a little bit more prominent (shown here in bold) and the utterance becomes metrical. The movement may be reinforced by pitch jumps between the stressed syllables, resulting in a spiky or glissando effect.

I **real**ly **think** it's **time** you **ought** to **go**.

The result is to make the utterance seem more emotional. You might be irritated (this is the third time you've suggested it) or concerned (you'll miss the train if you don't) or excited (the fans are waiting outside).

To make a sentence less rhythmical, the pitch, loudness, and rate all vary, and pauses intervene unpredictably.

I **real**ly - **think** it's **time** you - **ought** to - **go**.

I can imagine this being said with great feeling before a loved one leaves on a long journey. There may be additional effects:

the occasional stammer, gulp, or sob, perhaps. It's natural for rhythm to break up in this way when you're greatly moved.

Rhythmic effects provide an additional resource for public speakers. Listeners immediately notice when speech becomes more rhythmical or less rhythmical. An increase draws attention to the words that carry the strong beats, and the phrases that contain them. So when Obama says

> a government **of** the people / **by** the people / and **for** the people ...
>
> the **heartache** and the **hope** / - the **struggle** and the **progress** / ...

it's the rhythmical parallelism that is the basis of the dramatic effect. The phrases reinforce each other and the sequence becomes more memorable.

A decrease has an effect too. If your aim is to make an intensely personal statement, then a strong rhythmical beat would make it sound prepared and glib – insincere. By contrast, as we saw in Chapter 15, a broken rhythm reinforces personal emotion.

> I know that - my debt to them is beyond measure /

As with other prosodic features, it's important not to overdo it. It would be perfectly possible to add even greater emotion to that sentence by introducing extra pauses:

> I - know that - my - debt to them is beyond - measure /

But such a level of disturbed rhythm is best restricted to really intimate occasions, such as funeral orations. In other settings, where there's no apparent reason to show emotion, arhythmic speech is more likely to convey an impression of speakers being out of control or out of their depth, or just not being very good at speaking. It certainly doesn't give the impression of eloquence.

Rhythm goes hand-in-hand with pausing, as the transcriptions show. This is silent pausing, of course, not the filled pauses (the ers and ums) I described in Chapter 16. Experienced speakers know the value of a well-timed silent pause. And they know that different effects can be conveyed by varying the length of the pause. So what are the options here?

The basic unit of silent pause is a beat of the speaker's natural rhythm. If I'm speaking in a regular 'te-tum-te-tum' way, then my default pause will be, as it were, a 'tum':

te-tum-te-tum-te-tum [beat] te-tum-te-tum-te-tum ...

It's the predictable pause we use between sentences, or when there's a major grammatical break in a sentence:

John got home very late last night [beat] the car had
    broken down ...
There are two important points to make [beat] the first
    is ...

It's also the default in a list:

democracy [beat] liberty [beat] opportunity [beat] ...

When I'm transcribing speech (as in the examples in earlier chapters) I show the default pause with a single dash. A pause twice as long I mark with a double dash. A pause three times as long (or more) with a triple dash. And if the pause is shorter than normal, I show it with a dot.

The contrasts are subtle, but they can be very meaningful, especially in public speaking. We talk about a 'dramatic pause', for example, when it is noticeably longer than normal. It keeps the listener waiting, but not for too long:

And you know what he said? [beat] [beat] I can't go!

A three-beat pause is always possible in such narratives, but the speaker had better be sure the wait is worth the extra silence. And – the same old story – if the effect is overused, it begins to lose its impact.

In some contexts a long pause wouldn't work. We wouldn't expect one here, for example:

There are two important points to make [beat] [beat] [beat] the first is . . .

The long pause reduces the impact of the opening words. If the points are so important, we expect the speaker to give them to us without more ado. The longer the pause, the more the speech conveys uncertainty. Maybe the points aren't so important after all.

By contrast, a shorter pause than normal speeds things up:

John got home very late last night . the car had broken down . I was on my own . . .

This is breathless storytelling. The brief pauses convey urgency and excitement. You can't wait to tell the story. But the quick-fire sequencing shouldn't go on for too long, and of course it needs to be justified by a worthwhile ending. Why the excitement otherwise?

This kind of storytelling is common in everyday conversation. It often means no more than that the speaker is in a rush. But in public speaking, a series of sentences joined by brief pauses is unpalatable. Listeners lack the time to process them efficiently. It's very difficult to remember the content of a gabble.

So I would never leave a brief pause in an example like this:

There are two important points to make . the first is . . .

The content motivates a longer pause. Not only must the speaker take a deep breath at this point; the listener must too.

A deep breath. I meant that as a figure of speech. Some speakers might actually breathe in deeply. But would eloquent speakers ever want their breathing in and out to be heard? Sometimes.

Handling hecklers

Statler and Waldorf heckling the cast of *The Muppet Show*
from their balcony seats

A longer-than-normal pause can prompt an audience to do something unexpected. In particular, at public meetings it gives people time to heckle. There's especially a risk in leaving a dramatic pause after a rhetorical question:

Where are we going? —— I'll tell you . . .

Some wag is bound to shout 'Home' or 'Down the pub' or whatever. To avoid it, the pause needs to be kept really short, with a quick follow-up.

I've met several political speakers who welcome heckling, because they know they're good at producing a riposte. So they build into their speech moments of invitation, deliberately leaving the pauses long. If nothing happens, they move on. But if a heckle arrives, they have a prepared response at the ready.

20

Paralanguage

Prosodic variation is the foundation of eloquent delivery. This is because it's always there. We can't say anything without giving it a particular pitch, loudness, rate, rhythm, and pause. But prosody doesn't exhaust the range of effects we can convey with our voice. There are special 'tones of voice' that we introduce every now and then, and eloquence can make use of those too.

Whispering is a good example. We whisper when we don't want someone to hear us. In everyday life, the occasions are often conspiratorial, sometimes genuinely so, sometimes with mock seriousness – 'shhh, she might hear us', even though the person in question lives miles away. It might seem unlikely for whisper to ever have a role to play on the public stage, but I've often heard the mock effect, and used it myself.

I mentioned in Chapter 8 that I sometimes give a lecture called 'The Future of Englishes'. At one point I talk about how the rise of English as a global language is a relatively recent phenomenon. I refer to the 1580s, when people were saying that English was a worthless language because (a) it was useless to travellers abroad and (b) it didn't have a literature worth reading. When I develop the literary point, I say something like this:

What a bad time to be saying such a thing! We don't have many facts to go on, but one thing we do know is that in November 1582 a young man from Stratford-upon-Avon got married. The belief is that he then travelled to London for a career as a poet, actor, and playwright. And, if the latest research is to be believed, <u>he spent one night with Gwyneth Paltrow</u>, and as a result wrote *Romeo and Juliet*. ——

I usually move closer to the audience when saying 'if the latest research is to be believed', look conspiratorial, whisper the underlined bit, and say the final clause at normal loudness, ending with a crescendo.

It gets a good laugh. You can hear the audience reaction online in various versions of the talk. It's a slightly naughty joke, so the conspiratorial effect is appropriate. Audiences who have asked to hear this lecture are likely to know the movie *Shakespeare in Love*, and have heard of the star, so they get the joke straight away. And in case there are some who haven't, I add a brief comment about the movie, and suggest they watch it.

Whisper is an example of what phoneticians call a 'para-linguistic' feature. It's an isolated effect that is at the edge of language (*para* means 'above' or 'beyond', as in *parachute*). It's not like the pitch movements we use, which operate as a system of contrasts. It's just – whisper. Nor is it a particularly English feature. Whisper goes above and beyond any one language. Exactly the same effect could appear in French or Swahili or, I suppose, any language. (There may well be languages where people never whisper, but I don't know of any.)

There aren't many paralinguistic features, but when they do occur they're instantly recognizable and they immediately alter the tone of what's being said. Audible breath is another. A breathy voice is one that is approaching whisper but not quite getting there. You hear it most often when someone speaks after running or doing some violent exercise. The words are heard breathily within the puffing and panting.

That's a biological reason for breathy voice. There can be a linguistic reason too, when we're not out of breath but deliberately adding some extra breath to what we're saying, for effect. If I say 'Oh yes' in my normal full voice, it means what it says. If I say it in a breathy voice, I show greater emotional involvement. Some female film stars used to do this quite a lot on screen. (I've no idea if they spoke like that at home.) There's actually a web page on the Internet Movie Database headed 'Women With Soft Breathy Voices'. Top of the list are Marilyn Monroe and Jayne Mansfield.

Breathy effects are rare in public speaking, but they can be used to dramatic effect. I remember listening to a talk by a doctor who was pointing out the dangers of sunburn. He had just returned from a holiday abroad and had seen a beach, he said, where 'some of the people were sunburnt all over'. If had said this in his normal voice it would have been a simple statement of fact, and not especially memorable. But what he actually did was lean his head forward, open his eyes wide, as if in surprise, and made the last two words strongly breathy. They 'were sunburnt ALL OVER'. They really were sunburnt! The audience remembered that. I still do, years later, although I can't recall a word of the rest of the talk.

Other paralinguistic effects include constricting the throat a little to produce a husky or hoarse voice. That can express disparagement. You might add a touch of nasality or a creaky voice or extra resonance. Most noticeable of all is speaking through a spasmodic articulation, as when you laugh, giggle, sob, or cry while talking. Again, these effects are unusual in public speaking, but when they occur they're highly effective. Imagine a speaker fighting off tears or laughing in an apparently uncontrolled way – corpsing. The audience is immediately involved. The crying and laughing can be contagious.

Note I say 'apparently'. The emotions may bubble up naturally and sincerely, or they may be a controlled effect. Actors
learn how to switch these effects on and off. Public speakers can
do the same. Is the laugh that suddenly accompanies a story that
the speaker has told many times before genuine? Probably not.
But the effect on the audience is the same as if it were. The
speaker has made them *feel*. A widely quoted observation attrib-
uted to author Maya Angelou captures the point well: 'People
will forget what you said, people will forget what you did, but
people will never forget how you made them feel.'

There's no graphic convention to show paralinguistic effects.
All a novelist, for example, can do is write such things as 'Jane
replied breathily' and 'Mike said in a seductively husky voice', and
rely on the reader to recognize the effect and interpret the sentence
accordingly. And the same applies to non-fiction writers. It might
take a whole paragraph to describe a particular effect when in an
audio recording it would be there in an instant. That's why I made
so much use of the Obama speech earlier. If my description of his
eloquence was unclear, it's a simple matter to find the speech
online and relate my account to what actually happened.

Each of the effects I've so far described has a second dimension. I 'looked conspiratorial'. The doctor leaned his head
forward and opened his eyes wide. The effects are visual as well
as auditory. Corpsing doesn't come across so well on the radio.
The two dimensions complement each other. And because of
this, the visual element of communication – facial expressions,
eye contact, body movement, gestures – are also often brought
into the term 'paralanguage'.

Any book on public speaking will extend the mantra 'It ain't
what you say but the way that you say it' a stage further: 'It ain't
what you say nor the way that you say it but the way that you
look when you say it.' Some go into all aspects of appearance as
a result – such as the clothes you wear and the accessories you
use – but for me the aspects of visual communication to concentrate on are those that directly affect the linguistic features of a

speech. If there is to be eloquent spoken language, the accompanying body language needs to be eloquent too.

Visual eloquence doesn't mean gesturing all over the place.
That can be distracting. It means using the body to reinforce
the point you're making. The reinforcement can enhance the
message, as in the conspiratorial example. It can contradict
the message, in an ironic way. 'I'm really impressed by what the
Tories are saying,' someone (not a Tory) said in a TV interview
during an election campaign. But the straight face, the downward curl of the mouth, the depressed shoulders, and the flat
tone of voice said exactly the opposite.

Gestures don't work so well in some contexts. In an interview, they can appear defensive or even aggressive. If you're in a
small room, they can seem disproportionate. And if you're being
filmed, that effect can be even stronger. If the camera is showing
you in close-up most of the time, they can be intrusive. It's very
noticeable that in Obama's speech his hand gestures are minimal,
emphasizing only the important words.

What you do notice straight away, when you look at a
recording of that speech, is his head movement. He repeatedly
looks from side to side, taking in the whole arena. And this is a
strategy that any public speaker should also use. I remember a
church service where I was sitting halfway down on the preacher's right, and he looked only at the people on his left. I felt totally
left out. With all speakers, I want to feel that they know I'm part
of their audience. And the only way for that to happen is for the
speaker to look in my direction from time to time.

Note, I say 'look in my direction'. I don't mean 'look at me'. I
don't want the preacher gazing directly at me when he intones
'Thou shalt not bear false witness.' And if, a few seconds later, he
went on with 'Thou shalt not commit adultery,' and looked at
me again, I'd begin to wonder whether he knew something I
didn't. When people talk about making eye contact with an
audience, then, they don't mean eye contact. They mean: give the
impression of eye contact. This is best done by looking around

the audience as you speak, and looking slightly above them. I tell people to find a feature at the back of the room, just above the heads of the people at the back – such as a clock or a picture – and use that as their focal point. From the audience's point of view, wherever you sit, it appears you are looking at them.

It's very tempting to look at individual members of the audience, especially in a small room. You're making your points well (you hope) and the lady at the end of the second row is nodding appreciatively. So you keep looking at her. She may appreciate your recognition of her support, but the rest of the audience won't. You can lose an audience that way.

But the best way to lose an audience is to turn your back on them. You might think this is unlikely ever to happen, but you'd be surprised. I quite often see speakers with a screen behind them turn to look at the screen while they talk about what's on their slide. It immediately severs the connection with the audience. They lose what is being conveyed by facial expression. They may also find it more difficult to hear what's being said. Turning slightly to one side to refer to the screen is enough to draw attention to the visual content. But don't turn so much that your face is hidden. Look how the weather forecasters do it on TV, with a map of the weather behind them. They turn towards it, and gesture towards it, but you always see their face.

Of course, because this is such a fundamental rule of public speaking, it can be hugely effective if there's an opportunity to break it. But the timing has to be right. I remember a talk where a speaker made a particularly controversial point, the audience reacted vocally, so he turned his back, crouched down a little, and put his hands behind his head in a mock-self-protective gesture. Everyone laughed, and he got more sympathy that way than if he'd carried on full-face.

I read an article once on public speaking called 'Mind Your Language'. True enough. But you have to mind your paralanguage – including your body language – too.

The UX of content

UX is business-speak for 'user experience'.

In February 2015, Doug Kessler, the co-founder and creative director of Velocity, gave a keynote address at the TFM&A (Technology for Marketing and Advertising) event at Olympia National in London. He began by asking the question: 'Why do you think people are so afraid of emotion in B2B?' (B2B, or business-to-business, refers to commercial transactions between businesses, such as between a manufacturer and a wholesaler, or between a wholesaler and a retailer.)

He argued that, because of the social, personal, and financial risks in the decision-making process in B2B, it's an emotionally fraught process. People shouldn't think of the B2B buyer as simply a decision-making unit, but as a human being. Treat them as such and you get a better result. And the best way of showing them you're human too, he said, was through tone of voice, as this conveys your intentions, personality, and (brand) identity more directly than any other aspect of language.

Kessler was applying the notion of 'tone of voice' to written presentations, and to the whole business of how a brand appears in public, but his remarks apply with even greater force to oral ones. Tone of voice, he went on:

> has to carry a hugely important set of messages between the lines, so it is disproportionately powerful. It's a force-multiplier and a budget-multiplier, literally. It can sap away your budget depending on whether it's bland and dull. Or it can add hundreds of pounds worth of value if it has attitude and speed and it's fun to read. It's also a hugely underrated aspect of marketing in general, and certainly content marketing.

Tone of voice, he summarized, is 'the UX of content'. It's what people remember. Eloquence, it seems, pays.

21

Mind your technology

There's only one basic principle all speakers need to respect when it comes to preparing a speech that makes use of technology: prepare it on the assumption that the equipment won't work. We're supposed to be living in a technological age, but I wonder sometimes . . .

I'm talking here about problems relating to visual aids technology, rather than those relating to the use of a microphone which I described in Chapter 5. It can happen to the best of us. Technology treats everyone with equal disdain, and has no respect for the great and the good. In 2008, Senator Obama was on the campaign trail when his teleprompter suddenly broke down. It resulted in a hugely arhythmic and incoherent few moments. Political opponents, of course, were delighted, as it reinforced their contention that this was not only a man of 'words not deeds', but a man for whom even the words were a sham.

It may appear to be stating the obvious to arrive in good time to check that the technology works; but it's surprising how often this proves difficult to arrange – usually because the room is being used by someone else immediately beforehand. And there's a less obvious problem. You need to carry out your check before the audience begins to enter the room – something organizers often fail to appreciate. If you want your slides to have an impact, you don't want them seen in advance of the presentation. That can be difficult to arrange too, especially if an impatient audience is wanting to come in out of the rain.

Problems are often of management rather than malfunction. I remember attending a conference where the keynote speaker brought a large pile of transparencies to use during his talk. Before he began, he checked their order and placed them carefully next to the projector. As he prepared to show his first transparency, he realized the projector hadn't been switched on. He pressed the switch, the fan started up – and promptly blew his transparencies all over the front rows. It's difficult to regain composure and maintain a modicum of eloquence after such a happening.

Speakers have to be prepared for such eventualities. An alternative characterization of eloquence is being able to cope with the unexpected while you're speaking. A talk should be able to survive even the worst of technical breakdowns. The operative word in this chapter is 'visual *aids*'. The focus remains – or should remain – on the medium of speech. The visuals should contribute to eloquence, not conflict with it. Things can start to go wrong when speakers treat their visuals as a replacement for what they're saying, or make themselves totally dependent on them.

The principle underlying the use of visual aids is psychologically well grounded. People are likely to understand and remember more of a message if visual memory reinforces auditory memory. Research studies suggest that, three days after a solely oral/aural presentation, people recall about ten per cent of what was said; but if there has been a visual element in the presentation, this figure rises to a remarkable sixty per cent or more. However, for this to happen, careful thought has to be given to how the two mediums complement each other.

If photographs or other pictorial materials are being presented, with no linguistic text at all, the timing is critical, because the appearance of a picture immediately dominates anything being spoken. Controlling the projector yourself can help you get the timing exactly right; otherwise you need to agree a method of instruction with the operator ('Next slide, please'). Every picture needs its introduction. And when a picture goes up, it's wise to pause, to give the audience a chance to absorb it, before providing any further commentary about why it's there. A common failing is to have too many slides – a maximum of a slide a minute is often recommended – and to leave them up for too long. If they remain visible after you've finished talking about them, they become a distraction. Inserting a blank slide before the next illustration is an easy solution.

There are certain obvious requirements, but it's surprising how often they're not respected. The room needs to be blacked out, otherwise the audience will see nothing but a series of ghostly images. The slides have to be visible from all parts of the room – something that in local venues, such as parish halls or a hotel dining room, may not be possible to achieve. And if there is text rather than a picture, it has to be legible to those seated farthest away. The type size has to be large enough to be read, and this reduces the amount of information you can get onto the slide. The most legible slides are those that contain no more than three or four short points.

As with pictures, the audience needs time to absorb what is written. A slide immediately takes audience attention away from the voice, so there is no point in saying something critical at this juncture. There also needs to be a brief pause before you address what is on the slide, because people find it very difficult to process conflicting channels of linguistic information at the same time. We sometimes hear a protest in a multi-party conversation or panel discussion: 'One at a time! I can't listen to two of you at once!' The same issue arises in a presentation where there is a dissonance between what is being said and what is being read. Some of the audience will give priority to the audio channel; others to the visual channel; others will switch uncertainly from one to the other. Speakers need to think carefully about how to distribute their content when using visual aids.

Universally acknowledged to be the worst practice is 'PowerPoint karaoke'. This is where a text is put up on a slide, and the speaker then painstakingly reads it out, word by word. Most people, of course, have already seen what is on the slide as soon as it appears and have speed-read it, so that the spoken version is redundant. If it contains humour, the joke has been appreciated before it is said, so that any punchline loses its impact and receives only polite laughter. And because visual processing is always a little ahead of auditory processing, there's a constant tension between reading and listening that is counterproductive. Irritation levels often rise.

Visual aids are a good servant of eloquence, but a bad master. At their best, they provide a springboard that enables a speaker to convey a message in an interesting, immediate, and memorable way. For those who have never seen a picture of Shakespeare's First Folio or an original King James Bible – and if the speaker doesn't happen to have brought one along – the sheer size and weight of the objects can be appreciated through a picture. And there's no real substitute for a well-designed graph or pie-chart showing trends, such as a swing between political parties at an election, or a growth in sales of a commercial product. Good supporting visual material can help foster eloquence.

On the other hand, visual aids can impose a straitjacket that leads to the disaster I reported in Chapter 4, where an overrunning speaker had to rush through a series of slides in order to reach his conclusion. The unpredictability I mentioned above can arise from all sorts of causes. Even if your speech has been carefully prepared and rehearsed, a new thought may strike you as you speak, and you find yourself running with it. Or a prepared point may take longer to explore than you expected. Or an unexpected audience reaction or external event may take you off in a fresh direction. Or you have to start late because of an overrunning introduction. Whatever the cause, the consequence is a loss of time. And it's surprising how quickly a series of small time losses can lead to the sudden realization that you have only five minutes left and you have eight slides to go.

The point is a general one: even if you're using no visual aids, these factors can make time run away with you. Indeed, unless you are a hugely self-disciplined and well-rehearsed speaker, it's almost bound to happen. You will have to talk-trim. So how is the problem of time management best handled?

At the end of Chapter 9 I talked about the way an audience's attention span – typically around ten minutes – motivates a modular structure for a long speech. It is in fact a very natural way of proceeding when you first sit down and think about what you're going to say. You jot down a series of points as headings and then organize them into a logical sequence. You think about what you want to say under each heading, and estimate how long it will take to deal with it. A module is simply this chunk of time-related content. Through rehearsal – or repetition, if the talk is being given several times – you sharpen your sense of the time involved in presenting each module.

If a talk is planned in this modular way, it provides a mechanism that can be a lifeline for an overrunning speaker. Let's imagine a thirty-minute talk that has been structured as a series of eight modules: a two-minute opening story, perhaps, followed by a five-minute introduction, a ten-minute major theme, four follow-ups each taking three minutes, and a one-minute conclusion. That's thirty minutes, without any unexpected things happening.

But let's say that the major theme, or the first follow-up, or the attention-recharging lulls between modules take up more time than expected. You realize, twenty-five minutes in, that you have dealt with only two follow-ups. There are two to go. That's six minutes plus your conclusion. You have to talk-trim if you are to finish on time. The solution is obvious: omit one of the follow-ups. A modular structure, whether in your head or summarized in note form, allows you to see the options easily. You won't feel particularly happy about it, but because each module is self-contained the audience will never know. And if the talk is followed by a Q&A, there may well be a chance to reintroduce the omitted content later.

This last point is actually more important than it might seem to be, because a speaker's performance in a Q&A session can be a better index of eloquence than what has taken place in the preceding talk. Experienced speakers know how to manage Q&A sessions. If they have given a talk on several occasions, they know the kinds of questions that are likely to be asked, and have a repertoire of well-tested responses. Because they know their subject well, they have a further resource of mini-modules relevant to what they have been saying. If a question relates directly to one of them, they are home and dry. If it doesn't, the skill of the presenter is to make one of those mini-modules seem relevant to the question ('That's a very interesting question, and it reminds me of . . .'). For the eloquent speaker, there is no such thing as an unanswerable question (or statement – for not all interventions from the floor turn out to be questions). Equally, the skill of the practised political interviewer is to get the interviewee *not* to go off-topic in this way, but to 'answer the question'.

Inexperienced speakers always have too much material. I repeat what I said at the end of Chapter 4: they need to work out what they want to say, in the time they've been allotted, then think how they would say it if they had only half the time. They need to be prepared to cut, and know in advance which points can be cut without serious loss. (If reading a text, they should never need to cut, if they've timed it exactly in advance, monitoring reading-aloud rate, and allowing for pauses, possible audience reactions, and delays caused by overrunning introducers.) You may think that the minute-totals above are unnecessarily precise. They aren't. Being aware of the value of minutes and seconds in modules is part of the skill-set of an eloquent speaker, and is something that is increasingly demanded in online settings such as podcasts, which may be quite precisely time-delimited.

Also part of the skill-set is the ability to create a modular structure that suits the needs of any public-speaking situation. There are aspects of delivery that all public-speaking situations share, but there are also important differences of content and style. How many such situations are there?

Debating the point

With debates, time is of the essence. Speakers will be penalized or cut off if they exceed their allotted limit. In parliamentary debate, the overall time allocated to a debate governs the amount of time individual speakers have. A guaranteed number of minutes is given to the mover of the debate, the official Opposition speakers, and the responding minister. Others who have made known their wish to speak have time equally allotted.

If it's a long debate of four to six hours, the mover is allowed twenty minutes, the Opposition speaker twelve, and the minister replying twenty-five. Other speakers have up to ten minutes each. If the debate is shorter, the speakers' time is proportionately reduced. In a debate of two to three hours, the allocations go down to fifteen, ten, and twenty respectively. In a short debate of ninety minutes, it goes down further to twelve, eight and fifteen.

How do people keep to time? Digital clocks show the number of minutes that have elapsed since the start of each

speech. However, the Noble Lords it seems are not always diligent in this respect. In 2005, a Select Committee Report on the
Speakership of the House added a note:

> We suggest that it would facilitate self-regulation and be
> helpful to the Front Benches, the Member speaking and the
> House generally if the digital clock in the Chamber – as in
> the Commons – began to flash a minute before the time
> limit and rapidly once it was exceeded.

22

Talking about content . . .

It ain't what you say, it's the way that you say it . . . This seems to downplay content. Or, putting this another way, it suggests that you can talk about nothing at all, or say the greatest rubbish, and with good delivery people will be impressed and walk away thinking they've learned something. There's a certain amount of truth in that. I remember once getting into a real tangle at a university lecture. I was using notes, and they'd got muddled, so the exposition was, to say the least, confused, and at the end I was furious with myself. But then someone came up and said it was a really interesting talk and thanked me warmly. I had, it seems, expressed my poor thinking eloquently.

Content is not really the subject of this book, but there are certain aspects of content that do directly affect our judgement about the eloquence of a delivery. This is because the various situations in which we speak present us with constraints that govern the way we select and organize what we have to say. There's a branch of linguistics called stylistics that studies the way different varieties of language contain predictable elements that have to be used if the varieties are to be recognized. If we hear such phrases as 'legal English', 'religious English', 'sports commentary', and 'journalese', we can to a certain extent predict the kind of language the texts will contain. And the same applies to the phrase 'public speaking'.

Each stylistic variety in turn contains several sub-varieties, which are linguistically very different from each other. Legal language is found, for example, in contracts, wills, conveyances, and exchanges in court. Sports commentary has as many genres as there are sports to talk about. In each case the speaker or writer has to be aware of the demands of the situation and use language in a way that respects these needs. The right kind of content has to be selected, organized, and presented appropriately, recognizing any traditions of use and the formality of the occasion. Football commentary wouldn't suit snooker, and vice versa.

Public speaking is no different. It consists of a range of genres, all of which are governed by convention. Sometimes these conventions are so general that they allow the speaker a great deal of flexibility in what is to be said and how it can be said. At other times they are so strict that if they're not followed the speech would be considered a failure. All, of course, require the speaker to respect the general considerations I described earlier, such as knowing the audience, being audible, mastering technology, and keeping to time.

The number of public-speaking genres is actually quite small – fewer than twenty. Some – such as speeches at weddings – are well treated in the form of self-help guides, these days often online; but others receive little or no attention. I've compiled my own list below, based on my experience of each, and taking into account the kind of recommendations that are made in the self-help literature. (It doesn't include variations due to cultural diversity, such as those described in Chapter 7.)

Introducing a speaker

Main features: short, informative, formal.

Most introductions need only a minute; anyone who says 'Well, you've come to hear X rather than me' has gone on for too long. Informative here means identifying the speaker, the occasion, and the title of the talk, including only what the audience needs to know. Avoid saying 'This is someone who needs no introduction' and then introducing them at length. It's important to get the biographical facts right (including the correct pronunciation of the name, if it's at all unusual), which may involve asking the speaker in advance. Don't use the occasion as a soapbox for your own opinions. Use informality, including humour, cautiously, and only if speaker-related. Avoid asking the speaker beforehand what the speech is going to be about, but check any allusion to the content of the talk with the speaker, to avoid stealing any thunder. It never ceases to amaze me how often my introducer, having taken the trouble to read the book I'm going to be talking about, tells the very story I was planning to use to open the talk.

Thanking a speaker

Main features: very short, reflective, formal.

Very short means usually less than a minute. Reflective means referring to what the speaker said, to show you've been listening and appreciative (it's bad form to make a correction, even if you know an error was made). No need to give exaggerated praise: if the speech was good, it's unnecessary; if bad, it's insincere. It's impossible to prepare in advance, therefore, as spontaneity is important. Referring to any notes you made is acceptable, but not reading from a prepared text. If you've been invited to make a formal vote of thanks, but haven't been introduced, say who you are, and why you've been asked, so that the speaker and audience know.

Opening an event

Main features: short, focused, formal.

Up to five minutes, thanking for the invitation, saying why you agreed to do it (especially if there's some personal connection), and thanking the organizers (especially if they're volunteers). The content should be related to the occasion; this isn't an opportunity to talk at length about yourself, though the occasional jocular self-reference is appreciated, especially if you're a well-known personality. For fêtes, bazaars, and other fundraising occasions, emphasize the reason for the event and draw attention to those who will benefit. It's crucial to formally end by declaring the event open.

Presenting an award

Main features: short, informative, personal.

Short, yes, but not too short, as the occasion needs proper recognition – usually up to five minutes. The person's achievement (or achievements, if it's for a lifetime of service) needs brief recapitulation, as does the origin and character of the award (the donating body, the object being awarded). Check the exact name of the award. Say why you've been asked to make the award, and your feelings about the moment. Formality is variable. With some occasions, such as a retirement gift, the occasion can take on the character of a family gathering.

Receiving an award

Main features: very short, sincere, formal.

Usually up to half a minute. The moment is inevitably emotional, but speakers need to bear in mind that any excess of emotion can cause embarrassment and provoke later criticism (the Oscars syndrome). It's important to recognize the donating organization and to thank anyone who helped you to the position. Acknowledge others who may have been in the running for the award. Avoid saying 'I don't deserve this', even if you feel it; at best it sounds clichéd and at worst suggests a criticism of those who thought you did.

Making a toast

Main features: short, focused, formal.

If it's a loyal or patriotic toast, the name of the person being toasted is all that is required, said proudly and loudly ('The Queen!') – minimalist eloquence. It's important to get the phrasing exactly right, though, if there's an official name and traditional wording for a toast ('Rotary International, and peace the world over'). Give people time to repeat the toast before you sit down. If it's a social toast, such as to a couple celebrating an anniversary, length and formality are flexible, but two or three minutes would be usual. An apposite quotation can be effective, as long as it isn't so well known as to be a cliché. Toasts always end with the names of the people to be toasted.

Speaking at a school speech day

Main features: no more than twenty minutes, lively, anecdotal.

Many people have memories of interminable school speech days, and wishing the event was over. If it is your own old school, the obvious focus is on your role in connecting past and present, with liveliness added by personal memories and stories. If you are an outsider, there are parallels to be drawn with other institutions. Check with the headteacher if there's anything you're expected to say (such as asking for a school holiday). The audience is threefold: school staff and governors, parents and relatives, students. If you focus on the first two groups, only they will enjoy it. Focus on the last, and everyone will.

Giving an after-dinner speech

Main features: undemanding, self-related, witty.

The time varies greatly – usually no less than ten or fifteen minutes, but not much longer unless this has been agreed in advance (often the case with a celebrity speaker). If the event is in the evening, and especially when following other speakers, keeping the speech short is likely to be appreciated. The personality of the speaker is a critical element, so this is not an occasion to be self-effacing. Formality varies with the occasion, but even the most formal of occasions enjoy humour. Use of visual aids can be difficult, given awkward room-dimensions and round-table seating. Attention can also vary outside normal limits, especially if coffee is still being served while you talk and your listeners are being asked if they want it black or white. With a late-evening talk, even the most eloquent of speakers may be unable to stem approaching somnolence. Beware the effects of alcohol, which can make your speech seem to you – but to nobody else – to be supremely eloquent.

Giving a family speech on a happy occasion

Main features: informal, personal, emotional.

These are special occasions – such as a birthday, silver wedding anniversary, or engagement – where the enjoyment lies in the intimacy of the gathering. The content is formed chiefly out of memories and anecdotes, and speakers have to be prepared for good-humoured boisterous audience interaction. There's no fixed time frame, but most speakers don't go on for more than five minutes. There may be visual aids, in the form of photographs, video recordings, and memorabilia.

Giving a family speech on a sad occasion

Main features: formal, personal, emotional, focused.

Funerals, memorials, and other sombre occasions have no fixed time frame, though anything less than five minutes would probably be thought insufficient. The mood requires elevated words, which can often be taken effectively from literature, but private memories are also privileged. An element of nostalgic humour can lighten an occasion, and if the event is perceived as a celebration of a life, then virtually anything can be said, as long as it is focused on the individual.

Speaking at a wedding

Main features: short, informal, personal, witty, traditional.

With a traditional wedding, the three-speech format suggests a comfortable time frame of around five minutes per speaker. The father of the bride (or whoever is giving the bride away) speaks first, and toasts the bride and groom. The bridegroom replies on behalf of his wife, includes thanks to parents and organizers, and toasts the bridesmaids. The best man replies on behalf of the bridesmaids, in a speech that can be longer because there is more to do. In addition to any personal anecdotes (about the groom), there may be messages to be read from people who cannot be present – in which case, he needs to explain who they are (which may require some preliminary checking). Visual aids (such as embarrassing pictures of the groom) are appreciated, as long as everyone can see them. The best man may also need to act as master of ceremonies if there's no toastmaster there to do it. These days, the speech roles can be distributed more widely: to have two best men allows an opportunity for a 'double-act' speech, and the bride or a bridesmaid may take on a main speaking role. An important task is to ensure that everyone's glass is filled before a toast. This invariably improves the audience's perception of eloquence.

Speaking to a club or society

Main features: personal, focused, witty, interactive.

The time frame needs to be agreed in advance, but – if there's no preceding meal – is usually between thirty and forty-five minutes. Most such occasions expect an opportunity for questions. It is important to check if the time allotted includes this session or not, and also who will be in charge of it – the speaker or someone else. In particular, it needs to be agreed who is responsible for informing everyone of the critical moment that brings the event to a close: the 'last question'. (And then tactfully ending the meeting, if that last question turns out to be an interminable statement.)

Giving a lecture or conference presentation

Main features: fixed time, informative, formal, often technological.

Earlier chapters have addressed several of the issues that arise when people speak to industry conferences, make presentations at business meetings, or give academic lectures. The time frame is a given, but it needs to be checked whether there is to be a Q&A session, along with the other factors described in Chapter 4. The content will be affected by the talk status (whether the conference has a theme and whether the talk is billed as a 'keynote') and where in the conference schedule it appears – beginning, middle, or end – as this will influence the extent to which it is possible to refer to other contributions or conference activities.

Making a political speech

Main features: short, identifying, rhetorical, formal.

Political speeches have greatly varying time frames, depending on the occasion, though most are between fifteen and thirty minutes. There may be fixed time limits in particular settings established by tradition or circumstance, such as speeches at an annual party meeting or within a governmental assembly. In these cases, the individuality of speakers is secondary to the identity of their party or the cause they are supporting. Similar issues arise with memorial speeches that address significant historical moments, such as a battle or a peace.

Contributing to a debate

Main features: fixed time, interactive, rhetorical, semi-formal.

Whether you are proposing a motion, opposing it, seconding it, or contributing from the floor, there will be a time limit to be respected. The structure of the occasion is formal but speech style is commonly informal, bringing speakers closer to the audience. The aim is to make the best possible case to persuade, so all three methods of rhetoric described in Interlude 7 (logos, ethos, pathos) are used. The factual content of the argument is often enhanced by enthusiasm and humour. Debating manuals recommend that the focus of the speech should be on the opponent's arguments, not on the opponent as a person, and that the manner of delivery should be polite and self-controlled; but press reports of 'ill-tempered debates' show that speakers don't always respect the ideal of dispassionate deliberation.

Distance broadcasting

Main features: short, isolated, reactive, formal.

Speaking 'down the line' to a broadcasting station, from a home studio or by telephone, live or pre-recorded, differs fundamentally from all other public-speaking genres in that you inevitably feel communicatively isolated. You have no eye-contact with the interviewer, and no simultaneous visual feedback about how you're doing. Nor should you expect to receive vocal reactions (of the 'mhm' type), as radio interviewers know these sound intrusive. The situation is exacerbated if you're contributing to a panel where you can see none of the other participants. The interviewer is in control, so you have no choice other than to be reactive, as in a Q&A session – though, as there, you can turn the questions in any direction you want. At least you don't have to worry about how you look, and the pressure can be reduced by having notes available as an aide-memoire. Experienced radio presenters suggest speakers should forget the potentially vast and mixed nature of the listening audience, and imagine they are talking to just one person. Most interviews are short, around three or four minutes, so points need to be made as succinctly as possible.

Podcasting and vodcasting

Main features: variable time, isolated, proactive, variable formality.

Podcasts can be as varied as any traditional broadcasting programmes. Most informally produced podcasts are between five and fifteen minutes long, but ambitious ones can be an hour or more. They can be audio alone or with video (vodcasting). As the recording isn't live you have the option of redoing it or editing it. Retakes may reduce spontaneity, but they invariably improve fluency. As with any broadcast, you have only a vague idea of who will eventually be listening or watching, so your choice of content has to be proactive, full of conviction, and self-contained. With video productions it's important to check that there's nothing distracting (or embarrassing) in shot behind you, and how much of your body can be seen by the viewer (hand and arm movements are especially likely to be constrained). Keeping yourself in shot can affect your ability to speak naturally, especially if you're used to speaking with a lot of body movement. I usually end up feeling very stiff.

Making a live video presentation

Main features: variable time, proactive, pseudo-interactive, formal.

In addition to the factors just mentioned in relation to vodcasts, live video communication adds the element of technological uncertainty. Whenever I give a talk via a medium such as Skype, I always warn my audience at the outset that the connection might break, and that they should be patient if it does. When it is restored, you need to check the point at which your speech was lost, and be prepared to continue from that place. If the link is one where you can see the faces of some of the audience at the receiving venue, bear in mind that the reactions of those you can see may not be shared by others in the room. There's also likely to be an electronic lag, so that reactions to what you're saying reach you after a short delay. In a face-to-face talk, you can tell how long to pause after a joke before continuing with your speech as the feedback is simultaneous. With distance speaking, this feedback is missing, so you just have to guess whether your joke has been successful or not. The same point applies in a video conference: if you pause for too long after making a point, other participants will think you have finished, and they will chip in. Live video links provide a spurious impression of interactive reality.

Making an impromptu speech

Main features: short, informal, personal, reactive.

It doesn't happen very often, but if you attend occasions where you might be 'asked to say a few words', it's as well to be prepared, to avoid what would otherwise be uncomfortable and uncomforting waffle. Nobody will expect a crafted speech, but an anecdote, as part of your personal reaction to the event, is always appreciated. A small mental stock of stories is a useful resource – as long as they are recycled at intervals. An allusion to something from a recent daily newspaper or TV show helps ensure freshness.

In all of these genres, apart from the last, there's a choice to be made: is the speech to be spoken or written? The most effective deliveries, in terms of the scale of eloquence I outlined in Chapter 1, are those where speakers make no use of written material. But reading a written text aloud can still be supremely effective, as my Obama analysis illustrated, as long as it is properly managed. For speakers who don't have the services of a teleprompter or autocue – which means most of us – our text will be on paper, often on more than one page, held in the hand or on a lectern. These simple factors present the greatest challenges to eloquence, and require proper stage management to be overcome.

Autocues for all?

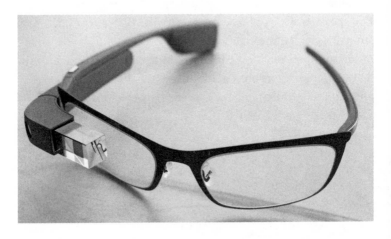

When I wrote that most of us don't have the services of a tele-prompter, I should have said 'not yet'. Smartglasses already exist that can project text into your field of vision, and it's presumably only going to be a matter of time before unobtrusive forms of these devices are routinely worn by speakers to make their notes privately visible, or to scroll down their text at a controllable rate.

23

Reading it

When reading a text aloud in public, the immediate challenge is how to foster an interaction with the audience. At several points in this book I've drawn attention to the importance of maintaining apparent eye contact with everyone. Turning your back on an audience is a definite disaster. So is keeping your head down while reading. Some of the worst reactions come when all listeners have seen is the top of a bowed head. 'I might as well have waited until I read it in the proceedings,' grumbled one conference attendee. 'At least I could skim the boring bits then.'

To leave the page and look around the audience is a risk. For a start, you have to be sure you can find your way back to where you were. Speakers develop their own techniques for doing this. A common one – if both hands are resting lightly on the lectern – is to use a finger to point to the location. But more important is to lay out the text in such a way that you can easily see where you are up to.

Layout is important for a second reason: it allows you to superimpose on your text the features of delivery that are prerequisite for eloquence. Chief among these is the memory processing limitation that I explored in Chapter 10. Complex speech is most comfortably processed in intonation-plus-rhythm chunks containing around five information units. Speaking aloud, likewise, is most comfortably presented in chunks of a similar length, as Interlude 10 indicated (p. 83). So when writing a text for spoken delivery, it's wise to be aware of this constraint. But, as pointed out in Chapter 10, it's a totally different task from writing a text that will only be read, for readers have the option of rereading. In a live presentation, there's no such thing as relistening.

Actually, I always like to read my writing aloud before publishing something – even in a book which is never going to be heard in spoken form. If there's too much information in a chunk of spoken text, this quickly becomes apparent because the rhythm falters and breath control deteriorates. A simple way of ensuring that this doesn't happen is to mark up the text into rhythm units or to lay it out in such a way that the rhythm units can be clearly seen. And if one of these units remains excessively long, rephrase. Here's an example from the paragraph you've just read.

First, the intonation-plus-rhythm units are shown by slashes:

> Actually, / I always like to read my writing aloud before publishing something / – even in a book which is never going to be heard in spoken form. / If there's too much information in a chunk of spoken text, / this quickly becomes apparent / because the rhythm falters and breath control deteriorates. / A simple way of ensuring that this doesn't happen / is to mark up the text into rhythm units / or to lay it out in such a way that the rhythm units can be clearly seen. / And if one of these units remains excessively long, / rephrase. / Here's an example from the paragraph you've just read.

Note that punctuation isn't always a reliable guide to rhythm units. There's no punctuation after *apparent*, for example. Some writers would insert a comma there, for that reason, but this option isn't available after *happen*, because one of the rules of modern English punctuation states that a comma should never separate a subject and a verb.

I know speakers who always mark up their texts in this way. Or parts of their texts. I do, whenever a sentence gets at all complex. Churchill did. The conventions vary a lot. I use slashes and continuation marks. Others might prefer highlighters, in various colours, or underlinings. And some use layout. Here's that paragraph with layout identifying the rhythm units:

> Actually, I always like to read my writing aloud before
>   publishing something –
> even in a book which is never going to be heard in spoken
>   form.
> If there's too much information in a chunk of spoken text,
> this quickly becomes apparent
> because the rhythm falters and breath-control deterio-
>   rates.
> A simple way of ensuring that this doesn't happen
> is to mark up the text into rhythm units
> or to lay it out in such a way that the rhythm units can be
>   clearly seen.
> And if one of these units remains excessively long,
>   rephrase.
> Here's an example from the paragraph you've just read.

It's now beginning to look like a poem, but I see that as a plus.

Note that the grammar of the language makes some rhythm-unit divisions more important than others. An opening adverb (*Actually*) or a short parenthesis of closure (*rephrase*) can be tacked onto another unit without loss. This is because their meaning is totally dependent on what follows or precedes. Indeed, to give them separate lines may actually foster a reverse effect: the speech can become vocally bitty. To avoid this happening, a third option is to combine the above two approaches, marking different lengths of pause (/, //, ///) and continuations (shown by ^). Here's one way of reading this paragraph:

> Actually, I always like to read my writing aloud before publishing something^ –
> even in a book which is never going to be heard in spoken form. //
> If there's too much information in a chunk of spoken text, ^
> this quickly becomes apparent /
> because the rhythm falters and breath-control deteriorates. //
> A simple way of ensuring that this doesn't happen^
> is to mark up the text into rhythm units /
> or to lay it out in such a way that the rhythm units can be clearly seen. //
> And if one of these units remains excessively long, rephrase. ///
> Here's an example from the paragraph you've just read. ///

Now the text is moving in the direction of a musical score. And indeed, some speakers take this idea further, underlining the words that need most emphasis, and even showing pitch movement. All this has illustrious and ancient authority. In Old English, the rises and falls of the voice in a sermon were shown by marks – one of the origins of punctuation. And in 1775, Joshua Steele included musical staves for his spoken examples in his suggestively titled *An Essay Towards Establishing the Melody and Measure of Speech to be Expressed and Perpetuated by Certain Symbols.*

I said above 'one way of reading'. It would be perfectly possible to read that paragraph aloud in a slightly different way. And in a highly rhetorical paragraph, such as one of Obama's, there would be many noticeable differences in the way it could be read. The techniques are helpful to discourse analysts, therefore, as they highlight contrasts in speaker style. But they aid the reader too, for positive and negative reasons. Not only do they provide cues to promote an eloquent reading, they help the reader to avoid miscues.

A miscue occurs when the way a text is laid out makes you read something the wrong way. You realize what's happened, and so you reread. Even newsreaders have slipped up in this respect: 'I'm sorry, I'll read that again.' A bad line-break is a common cause. A sentence appears to finish at the end of a line when in fact it carries on:

> This sentence appears to finish at the end of the line
> when actually it doesn't.

The risk is that you will use a falling tone on *line*, suggesting finality, even though there's no full stop there. (Full stops are the least visible of punctuation marks.) You're then left with a *when* clause hanging in the air. To avoid this, you can add a continuation mark after *line*.

Another very common miscue is caused by the conjunctions *and* and *or*. How is this sentence to continue?

> We can show the rhythm units using slashes or . . .

I might go on to say this:

> We can show the rhythm units using slashes or brackets.

Or it might be this:

We can show the rhythm units using slashes or we can use an array of specially devised punctuation marks.

If the *or* appears at the end of a line, there can be a moment of uncertainty. Is the next bit going to be a phrase (in which case there should be no pause after *slashes*) or a clause (in which case there should be, as the clause is quite a long one)?

Miscues are usually avoidable by a preliminary reading aloud of a text. It has to be aloud: silent reading won't bring them to light. Rehearsal also reveals other problems of layout, such as a page turnover interfering with a critical semantic point or pages inadvertently being out of order (ensure each page is numbered). Even the most accomplished of speakers can get into trouble if their fingers slip while page-turning or if pages get stuck together. If this happens at a point of paragraph division, the problem is trivial. If it occurs in the middle of a rhetorical build-up, it can ruin the effect. And opening a new paragraph on the last line of a page is never a good idea.

Rehearsed reading is critical. Nobody should ever read a text aloud in public without having first heard it themselves. Apart from anything else, the exercise gives speakers a sense of their limitations. How much visual text can you take in at a time and retain in your working memory while you speak it out? Some people can take in two or three lines of text without difficulty, especially if it's laid out well. Others have trouble retaining more than one. Familiarity with the text to be read can increase the amount of retention, improve speech flow, and avoid the distracting effect of rapid head-bobbing.

Rehearsal also allows the speaker to develop a sense of the text as a whole. Any effective speech is a coherent discourse. There is an arc of eloquence, and the various elements of the speech take their place within it. With short speeches, the arc is readily perceived. It will involve all the features I've mentioned earlier in this book, such as lulls, contrasts, build-ups, and points of climax, which are no less important just because a speech is written down.

The basic unit of discourse in a written text is the paragraph, not the sentence, and its identity must be respected when reading aloud. From an auditory point of view, perceiving a paragraph involves two features: an identifiable opening and an identifiable closure. The opening is always signalled by a rise in pitch, and the closure by a longer pause than those used to separate sentences. Radio newsreaders are adept at this. Listen to a news broadcast and note the way each new item of news is signalled by the opening words rising to a pitch level above the speaker's norm, after a longer-than-usual pause. The prosodic structure of a typical news broadcast looks like this:
An effective speech should display a similar structure.

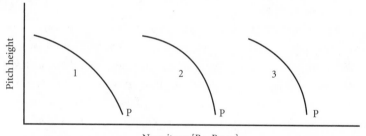

News items [P = Pause]

If a rise in pitch signals a paragraph opening, it's important not to introduce a similar pitch-rise within a paragraph, as this is likely to give listeners an auditory miscue. There needs to be a gradual decline in pitch over a paragraph, so that the last sentence is at the lowest level, running naturally into the paragraph-ending pause. For this to be most effective, paragraphs should not be too short or too long. There's no fixed rule, as length will be dependent on the nature of the content. But if a paragraph contains just one or two sentences, it won't give enough scope for the speaker to construct an effective auditory arc. Equally, it's difficult to maintain an auditory arc if a paragraph goes on for longer than five or six sentences – fewer, if the sentences are internally complex.

Larger than the paragraph are the major organizational divisions of the text – thematic sections and sub-sections. These need to be perceived too. The points of division are most obviously signalled by a longer pause than occurs between paragraphs. Many speakers reinforce their arrival by something external, such as a drink of water, a shuffling of papers, a new slide, or a fresh body posture. The text itself will provide clues too, of course ('Now let's move on to . . .'). But textual clues need to be supported by prosodic, paralinguistic, and extralinguistic effects if they are to be perceived most effectively. The best eloquence makes maximum use of all available communicative resources.

Finally, when rehearsing, it's good practice to vary your starting point, and not restrict yourself to 'beginning at the beginning'. If your speech has six modules, spend some time treating each as if it were a self-contained speech. The memory of doing this can inject an element of freshness at a point in a live presentation when your momentum might have declined. And it makes you better prepared for the unexpected distraction that might otherwise put you off your stroke.

It's something virtuoso musicians do, anxious to minimize the risk of losing their place in a memorized solo performance. If they're used only to performing the piece from the very beginning, it can be difficult to deal with a sudden distraction (such as a mobile phone going off) that interrupts their internalized sequence of notes. Less experienced players may have to go back to the beginning in order to continue. Practising a piece by starting in various places, it seems, reduces a player's anxiety and makes them more able to cope with the unexpected. When I put this to Welsh pianist virtuoso Iwan Llewelyn-Jones, he commented that, for him, this technique was 'a key factor – not only aiding memory, but strengthening the interpretation from several musical perspectives: structural cohesion, breathing and punctuation, focusing the arguments with dynamic shading and pacing'. In his choice of phrases, he could have been talking about eloquence.

'Reducing anxiety'. Nerves, in short.

Laying it out

The House will hv read the historic
declaration in which at the desire
of many Frenchmen,
and of our own hearts,
we hv proclaimed our willingness
to conclude at the darkest
hour in French history,
a Union of common
citizenship in their
struggle.

However matters may go in France,
or with the French Govt.
we in this Island and in the
British Empire,
will never lose our sense of
comradeship with the French
people.

If we are now called upon to endure
what they hv suffered,
we shall emulate their courage,
and if final victory rewards our
toils,
they shall share the gain,
aye, and freedom shall be
restored to all.

We abate nothing of our just demands.

Czechs, Poles, Norwegians, Dutch and
Belgians, who have joined their
causes with our own.
What General Weygand calls 'the battle
of France' is over.

The battle of Britain is about to
begin.

Upon this battle depends the
survival of Christian civilization.

Upon it depends our own British life
and the long continuity of our
institutions, and our Empire.

The whole fury and might of the enemy
must very soon be turned on us.

Hitler knows that we will hv to break
us in this Island, or lose the war.

If we can stand up to him,
all Europe may be freed,
and the life of the world
may move forward into the
broad and sunlit uplands.

But if we fail,
then the whole world,
including the United States,
and all that we have known and
cared for,
will sink into the abyss of a
new Dark Age
made more sinister and
perhaps more prolonged by
the lights of perverted
Science.

Let us therefore brace ourselves to
our duty, and so bear ourselves that
if the British Empire and
Commonwealth lasts for a
thousand years, men will still
say,

'This was their finest hour'.

Two examples of effective speech layouts. Both are from Winston Churchill. The speech 'paragraphs' stand out well, and the stepped indention provides the speaker with a clear indication of how the indication of the prosodic structure (p. 199) should be distributed. The short lines identify the rhythm units and the places to pause.

24

Nerve ending

Mark Twain, in an often-quoted remark, once asserted: 'There are two types of speakers: those that get nervous and those that are liars.' The exact words vary a little, depending on which source you use, but the sentiment is clear. Nerves are inevitable and natural, when speaking in public. There are no exceptions. So for those who say they suffer from them, the obvious question is how to deal with them, and that first means understanding what they are.

Nerve: the word arrived in English in the late fourteenth century, from Latin *nervus*, carrying over the physical meaning of 'sinew, tendon' and thus 'strength, energy'. *Nervous* too had a physical meaning at first: 'relating to sinews or tendons'. You could describe a bow strung with a sinew as being nervous; and if you had arms with prominent sinews, they could also be described as nervous. It's a point to watch when reading old texts: a 'nervous horse', in the 1600s, meant a strong, muscular one. It was only in the eighteenth century that the word came to mean 'anxious, apprehensive'.

Today, the word is used to describe a wide range of feelings, from the mildest of butterflies to a total paralysis, where the speaker is apparently unable to move, let alone speak. I have seen someone in this state, who had to be gently led from the stage after a minute or so of awful, immobile silence, followed by an announcement from the organizer apologizing for the speaker not being well. There is indeed an identified phobia – glossophobia – which is a profound fear of public speaking. As with any genuine phobia, it needs special help. That's not what most people mean when they say they're nervous about getting up to speak.

'Routine' nerves, if I may call them that, have milder but very noticeable symptoms, such as a dry mouth, a faster and erratic pattern of breathing, a sense of the stomach fluttering or churning, unexpected perspiration, shaky limbs. Some people feel nauseous; some find an urgent need to go to the toilet. Charlie Brown went further:

Nerves generally recede with experience – though I do know eloquent speakers who admit to being initially nervous every time they stand up. However, they usually then go on to talk about the importance of adrenaline, and affirm that the nervousness actually spurs them on. The important thing, they say, is to channel the energy released by the adrenaline into the performance. Several actors have told me that, without that adrenaline rush, they feel their performance was more lacklustre. But what does 'channelling energy' mean? And how do we actually do it?

Adrenaline is a word that's been used to mean 'nervous energy' since the 1920s. The way it works in the body is now well known.

When we encounter a potentially stressful situation, the brain sends a message to our adrenal glands (located on top of the kidneys) to release various hormones into our bloodstream, adrenaline being the primary one. It's an evolutionary adaptation that allows us to react to danger without life-threatening delay. The effect on us is often called the 'fight or flight' reaction; we have the option of fighting the danger or fleeing from it.

We need extra energy whether we fight or flee. The effect of the adrenaline is to make the blood vessels contract in most parts of the body, so that more blood is directed towards the heart, lungs, and muscles. Heart rate and blood pressure rise, sending improved circulation to the limb muscles that will enable us to act quickly. The air passages dilate and breathing rate goes up, allowing more oxygen into the lungs quickly, and giving us bursts of improved performance. As a result, less blood is available for parts of the body less directly involved in fight/ flight, such as the stomach.

The importance of the link between the nervous systems of the brain and the stomach, long recognized in Eastern medicine, is now very much appreciated in Western medical research, where the term *gut–brain axis* is frequently encountered. English vocabulary has also long suggested the connection, through such idioms as *gut feeling* and *gut reaction*. Adrenaline-induced variations in the tension of the muscles comprising the sensitive, smooth wall of the stomach produce the fluttery sensations we describe as butterflies. An adrenaline rush can also impede digestion, which can in turn produce feelings of nausea.

A comment often made by public speakers is that their nervousness disappears when they actually start talking. They say they are 'channelling the nervousness'. This is because the energy being built up in the body (for fight or flight) finally has a chance to be released. Adrenaline causes the body to release glucose, which raises blood sugar levels, the primary source of energy. If the energy has no outlet – because there's no real need to fight or flee just before a talk – it makes us restless and alters mood. Many speakers report feeling unusually irritable in the period leading up to their talk, or less sociable, not wanting to talk to anyone, and wishing the well-meaning chatty chairperson would shut up.

All this immediately suggests one trick that I know many public speakers use. Get rid of the energy. I've seen some engage in brisk physical activity – press-ups or arm swings – in the wings for a minute or so before being called on to a stage. Actors spend a great deal of time 'warming up' physically, loosening their muscles (including their vocal cords). Going to the toilet helps for that reason – not necessarily because there is actually any matter to excrete – but the getting there and back uses up some of that energy. Engaging in physical jerks isn't so easy during a dinner, sitting on a panel, or standing in a pulpit – though I don't deny that the effect of a vicar doing press-ups before a sermon could have a positive effect on a placid congregation – but there are alternatives. *Peanuts* again:

Deep breathing is the easiest alternative. This uses up a huge amount of energy, almost without the person realizing it. A slow and steady intake of breath, followed by a slow and steady release. There's no magic figure for 'slow and steady', as the time it takes us to breathe in and out varies according to our age and physical condition, but most people are comfortable with five or six seconds in, hold for a moment, and the same or a little longer out. Some speakers follow a specific formula, such as Andrew

Weil's four in, seven hold, and eight out.[23] Even just one such iteration, immediately before speaking, can turn a quavery voice into a confident one.

Deep breathing is just one of various relaxation techniques that nervous public speakers can use – and there's no shortage of books and online courses that offer guidance, from short-term measures to long-term advice about lifestyle. From a linguistic point of view there are some obvious preparations that can be made to anticipate symptoms. Dry mouth? Have a glass of water available. Sweating? Keep a handkerchief handy. Stomach gurgling? Eat a banana (a well-tried acting remedy). Stomach churning? Where possible, avoid making the stomach unnecessarily active through eating and drinking a lot immediately before the talk – though with wedding receptions and after-dinner speaking the situation is out of the speaker's control. Avoid alcohol, unless you are *very* sure of the way your body responds to it.

Above all, speakers need to reflect on the realities of their situation. It is not actually fight or flight. You are in no physical danger. Your audience wants you to succeed. They are on your side. They are probably thanking their lucky stars right now that it is you, not they, who are about to talk. They know they would be just as nervous, if not more so. In fact some may even be vicariously nervous, especially if they know you – being nervous on your behalf, as it were. When a speaker makes an audience laugh at the very beginning of a talk (Chapter 8), there is a collective relaxation.

That's why it is so important never to look nervous when standing up to speak. It is for your audience's benefit, not yours. That's why you should never draw attention to your nervousness at the beginning of a talk. The audience accommodates to it, and begins to feel nervous too. And – perhaps the most important piece of advice of all – if something goes wrong (a slip of the tongue, a misreading, a mispronunciation, a page out of order ...), that's why you should Never Apologize, or even mention the mistake. That simply draws attention to the error, which most listeners will not have noticed anyway. As jazz trumpeter Wynton Marsalis put it: 'The nerves are a problem on trumpet, because when you mess up everyone can hear it. Just remember most people are too polite to say anything about it. That should calm your nerves.' For 'on trumpet' read 'in public speaking'.

Nerves, in brief, can help, not hinder eloquence, and certainly should never be used as an excuse to get out of an opportunity to speak. There's no way I know to eliminate them completely – certainly no linguistic way – but they can be reduced by a build-up of the powerful antidote: confidence. And confidence comes from being in control of what you're going to say and how you're going to say it – the theme of several earlier chapters. In short: preparation and rehearsal.

If you speak regularly, take a tip from the acting profession: reflect on the way past speaking situations weren't as bad as you expected. Remember the sense of achievement that followed the applause, and hold on to that. Some actors have told me they can reduce their nerves by recalling the buzz that comes from repeated successful performances. This can help turn nervousness into that closely related state of mind: excitement.

There are other tricks. Here's one from Richard Branson, in a talk he gave in 2015:

> When you need to speak in front of a crowd, close your mind to the fact that you're on a stage with hundreds of people watching you and instead imagine yourself in a situation where you'd be comfortable speaking to a group. For example, imagine that you're in your dining room at home, telling a story to friends over dinner. I know it sounds a little corny, but try it. This trick has certainly removed some of the anxiety for me.

It's not corny. Broadcasters train themselves to think this way. They don't think of themselves as talking to millions. They imagine themselves talking to You.

Knowing that there are no exceptions can be a help – realizing we're no different from everyone else. Twain's joke, with which I opened this chapter, is actually a tiny exaggeration: some people are so in command of their subject and their audience that they don't get nervous as a rule, but even they admit to a degree of nervousness when asked to do something well outside their routine. The more experienced a public speaker we are, the less we're likely to be bothered by nerves, but they are always there, lurking in the wings, ready to jump out when an occasion forces us out of our comfort zone.

An annoying correlation is between great experience and great age. There comes a point (so I'm told) when we are less able to remember our lines, speak for long periods without hoarseness, and come up with the general energy that eloquence demands. Staying in the speaking business can thus become an increasing source of nervousness. Something like this is presumably behind the surprising admissions from well-known personalities we'd expect to be so used to speaking in public that they would have lost their nerves years ago. Dame Judi Dench is on record as saying 'I have worse nerves now, fifty-four years after entering this business, than when I started.'[24]

I know of only one exception to the statement that public speaking is not 'actual flight'. This happened at the Royal Institution in London, where there is a long-standing tradition of Friday evening discourses. It seems that when these discourses first began, in the early nineteenth century, a lecturer who had been invited to speak took fright when he entered the theatre and saw the elite scientists of London on all sides of him. He turned and fled. Since then, visiting lecturers have been closely guarded to avoid the same thing happening again.

In 1992 I gave such a discourse, and joined my hosts for dinner beforehand. With five minutes to go, I found a burly sergeant-at-arms behind me. He took me by the shoulder and led me into a side room near the famous steeply tiered lecture theatre. He then withdrew and locked me in. Four and a half minutes of deep breathing later, the door was unlocked, I was taken by the shoulder again and led to the closed double doors into the lecture theatre. As the clock struck its first stroke, he opened the doors and I was thrust into the room to begin my talk. Nerves become irrelevant when there's no escape.

Putting nerves to work

There are occasions when acknowledging your nerves, if you're unused to public speaking, can also help get an audience onto your side. Emma Watson went one further. The Harry Potter actress (Hermione) became the UN Women Goodwill Ambassador in July 2014, and later that year made an impressive speech at the UN headquarters in New York launching the HeForShe initiative for gender equality. Towards the end of her speech she mentioned her nerves, but used the moment to introduce a slogan:

> In my nervousness for this speech and in my moments of doubt I've told myself firmly – if not me, who? If not now, when? If you have similar doubts when opportunities are presented to you I hope those words might be helpful. Because the reality is that if we do nothing it will take 75 years, or for me to be nearly a hundred before women can expect to be paid the same as men for the same work.

15.5 million girls will be married in the next 16 years as children. And at current rates it won't be until 2086 before all rural African girls will be able to receive a secondary education.

The slogan might not have been perceived as such, when first heard. But it took on a powerful resonance when she used it again to end her speech. It was a 'Yes we can' moment.

We are struggling for a uniting word but the good news is we have a uniting movement. It is called HeForShe. I am inviting you to step forward, to be seen to speak up, to be the 'he' for 'she'. And to ask yourself if not me, who? If not now, when?

25

Homo eloquens

So, is the gab a gift? I might ask the question of any artistic form. Is painting a gift? Is singing? Is cooking? Clearly, some people are virtuoso speakers, painters, singers, and cooks. They must, presumably, have some sort of special gift. But that doesn't mean the rest of us are giftless. On the contrary: humans are wired for eloquence. We are *homo eloquens*. It is a potential in everyone. More than a potential. I've never met anyone who didn't show in their conversational skills that they are capable of eloquence. The problem is that most people don't think they are.

There's a huge myth surrounding eloquence. It's thought to be only for the gifted, or for the great and the good on prominent public occasions. All books on eloquence reinforce the myth, because they want to show the artistic heights that *homo eloquens* can reach. I'm no different. My chief illustrations have been of well-known figures talking at important events. So it's important for me to end by drawing attention to the selectivity inherent in such a portrayal. If eloquence is the summit of a mountain, it is a mountain that anyone can climb. And through the normal process of language learning as children we have all climbed some way up, without realizing it. The evidence comes from everyday conversation.

Several years ago linguist Derek Davy and I collected many examples of conversations that had been recorded without the participants' knowledge (they were told afterwards, and their permission to use the recordings obtained). The speakers were all adult, male and female, of various ages and widely different educational backgrounds, and the subject matter was wide-ranging – stories about family holidays, driving incidents, super-stitions … discussions about football, living in London, sex education … The material is now archived in the Survey of English Usage at University College London, but extracts were published in a book for second-language learners,[25] along with an audio recording (so my impressions can be verified, should anyone think I'm overstating my case).

Some of the speakers spoke for two or three minutes without a break, their words punctuated only by the occasional supportive vocalizations of their listeners. Every one of them, I would say, was conversationally eloquent. They were all natural storytellers. There was little sign of the conscious high artistry I described earlier in this book, such as the use of groups of three parallel constructions; but every speaker displayed the kind of fluent variations in pace, pitch, rhythm, and paralanguage that are the foundation of eloquent delivery.

I doubt whether any of them would be comfortable at being described as *homo eloquens*, because most people have an image of eloquence that is of the most highly crafted variety. When asked, they deny that they are or could be eloquent. They say the sort of thing I alluded to in Chapter 3:

> I don't have a good speaking voice.
> People won't like my accent.
> I've got nothing to say.
> People won't be interested in me.

I'm no Barack Obama [or some other well-known public figure].

I'm not sure where these notions come from. They might be revealed on a psychiatrist's couch. They all stem from imagination, not experience. Some people, indeed, may have had a bad speaking experience which put them off, but they are the exceptions. Most of those who have a negative self-image of their speaking skills have never actually tried them out in public.

In the days when I did research into discourse, I used to record a conversation, without the participants being aware that they were being recorded, and later play it back to them. They are invariably surprised about how fluent they are. They tell each other dramatic stories, repeat a lengthy joke with great facility, and in almost journalistic vein report the whole of what happened in the previous night's TV episode. If they can do this talking to one person, or two, without worrying about their fluency or their accent, then there's the potential to do this to ten, or twenty, or two hundred. The issue is one of confidence rather than linguistic inadequacy.

The question of accent isn't as critical as it once was, thanks to a greater experience of regional accents on radio and television. In the days when only one accent was heard and respected in the media (the so-called 'received pronunciation' of the upper classes in the south-east of England), the social pressure to use that accent on public occasions was considerable. Regional speech was considered uneducated and inferior. I've been told many personal histories of how people went to elocutionists in order to improve their speaking voice – which usually meant getting rid of their regional accent. Today, people can still go to voice coaches to help them improve their speaking skills, but the emphasis is now on clarity and fluency and breath control, not on accent. It could hardly be otherwise when many leading BBC radio and television presenters are daily heard speaking with identifiable regional voices, and local broadcasting stations routinely display the accents of their own communities. Similar diversity is now the norm all over the English-speaking world.

Having said that, it has to be recognized that old attitudes take a long time to die out. Criticism of regional voices can still be encountered, and there is still a fear of being judged negatively simply because of accent. I've talked to many students taking part in inter-schools debating competitions, such as those organized by the English-Speaking Union in the UK, and have been struck by how often they are fearful that their regional accent will lose them marks. I try to reassure them – having judged such a competition once myself, and knowing several of the present-day judges – that their fear is totally without foundation. But it is nonetheless there.

Another myth lies behind the self-denigrating comments that 'I've got nothing to say' and 'People won't be interested in me'. Everyone has got something to say – not just because we all have our own opinions about things, but because life experiences differ. No two people have the same upbringing. No two people have lived in exactly the same places. No two collectors have the same collection. Everyone has an interest they can and do talk about, and on which they can offer a unique perspective. It might be football, racing cars, knitting, gardening, travel, *The Simpsons* ... or Shakespeare, local politics, climate change ... Out there are people who will indeed be 'interested in me'. The issue is one of opportunity to expound rather than lack of knowledge.

And having said that, we have to recognize that anything we like talking about can be enhanced by doing some research. None of us has all the facts of our favourite topic at our fingertips. And we never fail to learn something new when we spend a short time delving into it further. Once upon a time, this would require a trip to the local library. Today, the world of knowledge is in our living rooms, thanks to the internet. And if we are not electronically connected at home, the local library will almost certainly provide an alternative means of accessing online services – as well as providing enquirers with excellent advice about what is available on their topic and where it can be found. Librarians are the unsung heroes behind many an eloquent performance.

What about the last comment above: 'I'm no Barack Obama'? Comparisons with famous figures actually have a value, if they're turned into a learning tool. It's possible to learn a great deal from the eloquence techniques that others use – from Barack Obama to our own Uncle Joe or Auntie Ellen – as long as we don't try to be an exact copy, but assimilate them into our own style. There are illustrious precedents. Winston Churchill, in the years before he became known for his oratory, read all the major speeches of the past and often visited the public gallery of the House of Commons to listen to the speeches of his contemporaries. The outcome was not a copy of any of them, but a unique personal style.

When Churchill was twenty-two, he wrote an essay called 'The Scaffolding of Rhetoric': 'Of all the talents bestowed upon men, none is so precious as the gift of oratory. He who enjoys it wields a power more durable than that of a great king. He is an independent force in the world.' Or she. Churchill was thinking of the great orators of history, the vocal virtuosi. Eventually he would join their ranks himself. But he had to work hard to do so. So do those who become great rappers and talk-show hosts. So do we all. As the American essayist Ralph Waldo Emerson reassuringly observed, 'All the great speakers were bad speakers at first.'[26]

We're helped, of course, if schools foster eloquence. Some schools make a big thing of it. I was struck by the way sixteen-year-old Ivo Delingpole described the role of his school in this respect, in an article called 'How Eton Works':

> to succeed at Eton you do have to use a certain amount
> of persuasiveness, whether it's arguing your case to the

headmaster when you've done something wrong and you've been put on 'The Bill' (report), convincing your 'beak' (teacher) not to give you a long 'EW' (piece of homework), or talking people into coming to your house play when they might have something better to do . . .

People often say that Etonians are recognisable because of the confidence they exude. I suppose it comes from ease in conversation. From what I've seen, Etonians are brilliant at buttering people up. There are lots of opportunities to practise it. Whether it be dinner in your housemaster's private dining room, taking a visiting speaker out, or cooking supper at your tutor's, you're often participating in intelligent conversation with grown-ups.

And he draws an interesting parallel:

When you find yourself on 'The Bill', trying to justify your actions to the headmaster in the oldest schoolroom in the country, it's eerily similar to arguing in court.[27]

We mustn't fall into the trap of thinking that this kind of thing is only possible in the top public schools. Eton is by no means alone in fostering this kind of daily eloquence; but it's certainly not the norm in most schools. Some do have debating societies and go in for national competitions. It ought to be 'all'. It should be standard practice in any school to have a debating society, or at least a forum where students can engage in supervised discussion, with everyone having a turn, on topics that are important to them. Eloquence needs to be valued as an end in itself; and if appreciation of what it is hasn't come naturally from the kind of home environment I described in my Prologue, then it needs to be carefully nurtured in school.

In the end, eloquence comes down to the two themes that permeate this book: preparation and rehearsal. It applies to all the forms and levels of eloquence that I introduced in my opening chapter, whether the result of reading aloud, being assisted by notes and technology, or being apparently spontaneous. The 'apparently' is important. As Mark Twain remarked in a speech to the Whitefriars Club in 1899: 'Impromptu speaking ... That is a difficult thing. I used to begin about a week ahead, and write out my impromptu speech and get it by heart.' Oscar Wilde summed it up: 'Spontaneity is a meticulously prepared art.'

I believe that anyone with normal language skills has the gift of the gab – that is, they have a natural ability to achieve a level of effective and appreciated eloquence, once they devote time and energy to proper preparation and rehearsal. And the first step in that process, to my mind, is to understand, in the words of my subtitle, 'how eloquence works'.

That simple 'how' question covers so much. Whatever the occasion – family and friends, clubs and societies, schools and churches, lectures and conferences, speeches and debates, broadcasts and podcasts – we've seen it raise practical considerations of time-keeping, microphone technique, and audience awareness. It draws attention to tried and tested performance considerations, such as the rule of three, end-weight, and order of mention – strategies that make the speaker more effective and the listener's task easier. And it makes us appreciate the vocal techniques that are intimately involved in effective delivery, such as speech rate, rhythm, and intonation. All of us. From the uncertain first-timer to the talented old hand, everyone can benefit from an understanding of what really lies behind 'the gift of the gab'.

Obama's victory speech delivered at Grant Park, Chicago, 4 November 2008

This is a transcription of the entire speech used as the main example in Chapter 9 and following. In those chapters, to aid ease of reading, I used normal sentence capitalization and punctuation, such as is found in the CNN transcript of the speech. However, it can be misleading to write out a speech in this way without seeing the original, so below I put everything in lower-case, apart from proper names and the pronoun 'I', and replace punctuation by representing Obama's main pauses from shortest (-) to longest (---), the latter often of some length because of crowd cheering. I also transcribe the few non-fluencies. I don't retain the CNN paragraphing – which breaks the speech down into far smaller paragraphs than, say, the BBC transcript does – and I make corrections in a few places where every transcript I have seen has made errors. The speech is easily viewable in various locations online.

hello Chicago ---

if there - is anyone out there -- who still doubts - that America is a place where - all things are possible -- who still wonders - if the dream of our founders is alive in our time -- who still questions - the power of our democracy -- tonight is your answer ---

it's - the answer told by lines that stretched around schools and churches -- in numbers this nation has never seen -- by people who waited three hours and four hours -- many for the first time in their lives -- because they believed that this time - must be different -- that their voices - could be that difference --

it's the answer spoken by young and old -- rich and poor -- Democrat and Republican -- black white -- Hispanic Asian Native American gay straight - disabled and not disabled - Americans who sent a message to the world - that we have never been - just a collection of individuals or a collection of red states and blue states - we are and always will be the United States of America ---

--- it's the answer - th that - led those - who've been told for so long - by so many to be cynical - and fearful - and doubtful about what we can achieve -- to put their hands on the arc of history -- and bend it once more toward - the hope of a better day -- it's been a long time coming - but tonight - because of what we did on this day - in this election - at this defining moment - change has come to America ---

a little bit earlier this evening - I I received - an extraordinarily gracious call from - Senator McCain --- Senator McCain fought long and hard in this campaign -- and he's - fought even longer and harder - for the country that he loves -- he has endured sacrifices for America - that most of us cannot begin to imagine -- we are better off for the service rendered by this brave and selfless - leader -- I congratulate him -- I congratulate Governor Palin - for all that they've achieved - and I look forward to working with them - to renew this nation's promise in the months ahead ---

I want to thank - my partner in this journey -- a man who campaigned from his heart - and spoke for the men and women he grew up with on the streets of Scranton - and rode with on the train home to Delaware - the vice president-elect of the United States Joe Biden ---

and I would not be standing here - tonight without - the unyielding support - of my best friend - for the last 16 years - the rock of our family - the love of my life - the nation's next first lady - Michelle Obama ---

Sasha and Malia -- I love you both more than you can imagine - and you have earned the new puppy that's coming with us to the White House ---

and while - she's no longer with us -- I know my grandmother's watching -- along with the family that made me who I am -- I miss them tonight -- I know that - my debt to them is beyond measure --

to my sister Maya - my sister Auma - all my other brothers and sisters - thank you so much for all the support that you've given me - I am grateful to them ---

to my campaign manager - David Plouffe --- the unsung hero of this campaign who built the best -- the best political campaign I think in the history of the United States of America --- to my - chief strategist David Axelrod -- who has been -- a partner with me every step of the way - to the best campaign team ever assembled in the history of politics - you made this happen - and I am forever grateful -- for what you've sacrificed to get it done ---

but above all -- I will never forget who this victory truly belongs to -- it belongs to you -- it belongs to you --

I was never the likeliest candidate for this office --- we didn't start - with much money or many endorsements -- our campaign was not - hatched in the halls of Washington - it began in the backyards of Des Moines - and the living rooms of Concord - and the front porches of Charleston -- it was built by working men and women who dug into what little savings they had to give 5 dollars - and 10 dollars - and 20 dollars to the cause -- it grew strength from the young people who rejected the myth of their generation's apathy -- who left their homes and their families for jobs that offered little pay and less sleep -- it drew strength from the not-so-young people - who braved the bitter cold and - scorching heat to knock on doors of perfect strangers - and from the millions of Americans who volunteered and organized - and proved that more than two centuries later a government of the people, by the people and for the people has not perished from the Earth - this is your victory ---

I know you didn't do this just to win an election - I know you didn't - do it for me -- you did it because you understand the enormity of the task that lies ahead -- for even as we celebrate tonight - we know the challenges that tomorrow will bring - are the greatest of our lifetime -- two wars -- a planet in peril -- the worst financial crisis in a century -- even as we stand here tonight we know there are brave Americans - waking up in the deserts of Iraq - and the mountains of Afghanistan to risk their lives for us -- there are mothers and fathers who will lie awake after their children fall asleep and wonder - how they'll make the mortgage - or pay their doctors' bills - or save enough for their child's college education -- there's new energy to harness -- new jobs to be created - new schools to build - and threats to meet - alliances to repair -- the road ahead will be long -- our climb will be steep -- we may not get there in one year or even in one term -- but America - I have never been more hopeful - than I am tonight that we will get there - I promise you - we as a people will get there ---

CROWD: yes we can [repeatedly]

there will be setbacks -- and false starts -- there are many who won't agree with every decision or policy I make as president -- and we know the government can't solve every problem -- but I will always be honest with you about the challenges we face -- I will listen to you - especially when we disagree -- and above all I will ask you to join in the work of remaking this nation - the only way it's been done in America for 221 years - block by block - brick by brick - calloused hand by calloused hand -- what began 21 months ago - in the depths of winter - cannot end on this autumn night --

this victory alone is not the change we seek - it is only the chance for us to make that change - and that cannot happen if we go back to the way things were - it can't happen without you - without a new spirit of service - a new spirit -- of sacrifice -- so let us summon a new spirit - of patriotism - of responsibility - where each of us resolves to pitch in - and work harder and look - after not only ourselves but each other -- let us remember that if this financial crisis taught us anything - it's that we cannot have a thriving Wall Street while Main Street suffers -- in this country we rise or fall as one nation - as one people -- let's resist the temptation to fall back on the same - partisanship and pettiness - and immaturity that has poisoned our politics for so long --

let's remember that it was a man from this state - who first carried the banner of the Republican Party to the White House -- a party founded on the values of self-reliance - and individual liberty - and national unity -- those are values that we all share - and while the Democratic Party has won a great victory tonight - we do so with a measure of humility -- and determination to heal the divides - that have held back our progress --- as Lincoln said to a nation far more divided than ours -- 'we are not enemies but friends -- though passion may have strained - it must not break our bonds of affection' -- and to those Americans who - whose support I have yet to earn - I may not have won your vote tonight - but I hear your voices - I need your help - and I will be your president too ---

and all those watching tonight from beyond our shores - from parliaments and palaces - to those who are huddled around radios in the forgotten corners of the world - our stories are singular but our destiny is shared - and a new dawn of American leadership is at hand --- to those -- to those who would tear the world down - we will defeat you -- to those who seek peace and security - we support you -- and to all those who have wondered if America's beacon still burns as bright - tonight we proved once more that the true strength of our nation comes not from the might of our arms or the scale of our wealth but from the enduring power of our ideals - democracy - liberty - opportunity - and unyielding hope --- that's the true genius of America -- that America can change -- our union can be perfected -- and what we've already achieved gives us hope for what we can and must achieve tomorrow --

this election had many firsts - and many stories that will be told for generations but - one that's on my mind tonight's about a woman - who cast her ballot in Atlanta -- she is a lot like the millions of others who stood in line to make their voice heard in this election - except for one thing - Ann Nixon Cooper is 106 years old ---

she was born just a generation past slavery - a time when there were no cars on the road or planes in the sky - when someone like her couldn't vote for two reasons because she was a woman - and because of the color of her skin -- and tonight - I think about all that she's seen throughout her century in America -- the heartache and the hope - the struggle and the progress - the times we were told that we can't - and the people who pressed on with that American creed 'yes we can' --

at a time when women's voices were silenced and their hopes dismissed - she lived to see them stand up and speak out and reach for the ballot - yes we can --

when there was despair in the Dust Bowl and - depression across the land - she saw a nation conquer fear itself with a New Deal - new jobs - a new sense of common purpose - yes we can --

CROWD: yes we can

when the bombs fell on our harbor - and tyranny threatened the world she was there to witness a generation rise to greatness - and a democracy was saved - yes we can --

CROWD: yes we can

she was there for the buses in Montgomery - the hoses in Birmingham a bridge in Selma - and a preacher from Atlanta who told a people that 'we shall overcome' - yes we can ---

CROWD: yes we can

a man touched down on the moon - a wall came down in Berlin - a world was connected by our own science and imagination - and this year - in this election - she touched her finger to a screen - and cast her vote - because after 106 years in America - through the best of times and the darkest of hours she knows how America can change - yes we can --

CROWD: yes we can

America - we have come so far - we have seen so much - but there's so much more to do -- so tonight - let us ask ourselves - if our children should live to see the next century - if my daughters should be so lucky to live as long as Ann Nixon Cooper - what change will they see? - what progress will we have made? --

this is our chance to answer that call - this is our moment - this is our time - to put our people back to work and open doors of opportunity for our kids - to restore prosperity and promote the cause of peace - to reclaim the American dream and reaffirm that fundamental truth that out of many we are one - that while we breathe we hope - and where we are met with cynicism and doubt and those who tell us that we can't - we will respond with that timeless creed that sums up the spirit of a people - yes we can --

CROWD: yes we can

thank you - God bless you - and may God bless the United States of America

Martin Luther King's speech delivered at the March on Washington, 28 August 1963

The speech is easily viewable in various locations online.

I am happy to join with you today in what will go down in history as the greatest demonstration for freedom in the history of our nation.

Five score years ago, a great American, in whose symbolic shadow we stand today, signed the Emancipation Proclamation. This momentous decree came as a great beacon light of hope to millions of Negro slaves who had been seared in the flames of withering injustice. It came as a joyous daybreak to end the long night of their captivity.

But one hundred years later, the Negro still is not free. One hundred years later, the life of the Negro is still sadly crippled by the manacles of segregation and the chains of discrimination. One hundred years later, the Negro lives on a lonely island of poverty in the midst of a vast ocean of material prosperity. One hundred years later, the Negro is still languished in the corners of American society and finds himself in exile in his own land. So we have come here today to dramatize a shameful condition.

In a sense we've come to our nation's Capital to cash a check. When the architects of our republic wrote the magnificent words of the Constitution and the Declaration of Independence, they were signing a promissory note to which every American was to fall heir.

This note was a promise that all men, yes, black men as well as white men, would be guaranteed the unalienable rights of life, liberty, and the pursuit of happiness.

It is obvious today that America has defaulted on this promissory note insofar as her citizens of color are concerned. Instead of honoring this sacred obligation, America has given the Negro people a bad check; a check which has come back marked 'insufficient funds.'

But we refuse to believe that the bank of justice is bankrupt. We refuse to believe that there are insufficient funds in the great vaults of opportunity of this nation. So we have come to cash this check – a check that will give us upon demand the riches of freedom and the security of justice.

We have also come to this hallowed spot to remind America of the fierce urgency of now. This is no time to engage in the luxury of cooling off or to take the tranquilizing drug of gradualism.

Now is the time to make real the promises of democracy. Now is the time to rise from the dark and desolate valley of segregation to the sunlit path of racial justice. Now is the time to lift our nation from the quicksands of racial injustice to the solid rock of brotherhood. Now is the time to make justice a reality for all of God's children.

It would be fatal for the nation to overlook the urgency of the moment. This sweltering summer of the Negro's legitimate discontent will not pass until there is an invigorating autumn of freedom and equality. Nineteen sixty-three is not an end, but a beginning. Those who hope that the Negro needed to blow off steam and will now be content will have a rude awakening if the nation returns to business as usual. There will be neither rest nor tranquility in America until the Negro is granted his citizenship rights. The whirlwinds of revolt will continue to shake the foundations of our nation until the bright day of justice emerges.

But there is something that I must say to my people who stand on the warm threshold which leads into the palace of justice. In the process of gaining our rightful place we must not be guilty of wrongful deeds. Let us not seek to satisfy our thirst for freedom by drinking from the cup of bitterness and hatred. We must forever conduct our struggle on the high plane of dignity and discipline. We must not allow our creative protest to degenerate into physical violence. Again and again we must rise to the majestic heights of meeting physical force with soul force.

The marvelous new militancy which has engulfed the Negro community must not lead us to a distrust of all white people, for many of our white brothers, as evidenced by their presence here today, have come to realize that their destiny is tied up with our destiny. And they have come to realize that their freedom is inextricably bound to our freedom. We cannot walk alone.

And as we walk, we must make the pledge that we shall always march ahead. We cannot turn back. There are those who are asking the devotees of civil rights, 'When will you be satisfied?'

We can never be satisfied as long as the Negro is the victim of the unspeakable horrors of police brutality.

We can never be satisfied as long as our bodies, heavy with the fatigue of travel, cannot gain lodging in the motels of the highways and the hotels of the cities.

We cannot be satisfied as long as the Negro's basic mobility is from a smaller ghetto to a larger one.

We can never be satisfied as long as our children are stripped of their selfhood and robbed of their dignity by signs saying 'for whites only'.

We cannot be satisfied as long as a Negro in Mississippi cannot vote and a Negro in New York believes he has nothing for which to vote.

No, no, we are not satisfied, and we will not be satisfied until justice rolls down like waters and righteousness like a mighty stream.

I am not unmindful that some of you have come here out of great trials and tribulations. Some of you have come fresh from narrow jail cells. Some of you have come from areas where your quest for freedom left you battered by the storms of persecution and staggered by the winds of police brutality. You have been the veterans of creative suffering. Continue to work with the faith that unearned suffering is redemptive.

Go back to Mississippi, go back to Alabama, go back to South Carolina, go back to Georgia, go back to Louisiana, go back to the slums and ghettos of our northern cities, knowing that somehow this situation can and will be changed. Let us not wallow in the valley of despair.

I say to you today, my friends, so even though we face the difficulties of today and tomorrow, I still have a dream. It is a dream deeply rooted in the American dream.

I have a dream that one day this nation will rise up and live out the true meaning of its creed: 'We hold these truths to be self-evident; that all men are created equal.'

I have a dream that one day on the red hills of Georgia the sons of former slaves and the sons of former slave owners will be able to sit down together at the table of brotherhood.

I have a dream that one day even the state of Mississippi, a state sweltering with the heat of injustice, sweltering with the heat of oppression, will be transformed into an oasis of freedom and justice.

I have a dream that my four little children will one day live in a nation where they will not be judged by the color of their skin but by the content of their character.

I have a dream today.

I have a dream that one day down in Alabama, with its vicious racists, with its governor having his lips dripping with the words of interposition and nullification, that one day right down in Alabama little black boys and black girls will be able to join hands with little white boys and white girls as sisters and brothers.

I have a dream today.

I have a dream that one day every valley shall be exalted, every hill and mountain shall be made low, the rough places will be made plain, and the crooked places will be made straight, and the glory of the Lord shall be revealed, and all flesh shall see it together.

This is our hope. This is the faith that I will go back to the South with. With this faith we will be able to hew out of the mountain of despair a stone of hope. With this faith we will be able to transform the jangling discords of our nation into a beautiful symphony of brotherhood.

With this faith we will be able to work together, to pray together, to struggle together, to go to jail together, to stand up for freedom together, knowing that we will be free one day.

This will be the day when all of God's children will be able to sing with new meaning, 'My country 'tis of thee, sweet land of liberty, of thee I sing. Land where my fathers died, land of the Pilgrims' pride, from every mountainside, let freedom ring.'

And if America is to be a great nation, this must become true.

So let freedom ring from the prodigious hilltops of New Hampshire.

Let freedom ring from the mighty mountains of New York.

Let freedom ring from the heightening Alleghenies of Pennsylvania.

Let freedom ring from the snow-capped Rockies of Colorado.

Let freedom ring from the curvaceous slopes of California.

But not only that; let freedom ring from the Stone Mountain of Georgia.

Let freedom ring from Lookout Mountain of Tennessee.

Let freedom ring from every hill and molehill of Mississippi.

From every mountainside, let freedom ring.

And when this happens, and when we allow freedom ring, when we let it ring from every village and every hamlet, from every state and every city, we will be able to speed up that day when all of God's children, black men and white men, Jews and gentiles, Protestants and Catholics, will be able to join hands and sing in the words of the old Negro spiritual, 'Free at last! Free at last! Thank God Almighty, we are free at last!'

Endnotes

1. Denis Donoghue, *On Eloquence*, New Haven and London: Yale University Press, 2008, p. 154.
2. Tenor Films, 'The Bertsolaris: Discover the Basque Country', https://vimeo.com/106061107, accessed 24 November 2015.
3. Cicero, *Orator*, 17.56 and 3.213.
4. Quintilian, *Institutes of Oratory*, Book 11, Chapter 3.
5. Aristotle, *Rhetoric*, Book 3, Chapter 1.
6. Sam Leith, *You Talkin' To Me? Rhetoric from Aristotle to Obama*, London: Profile Books, 2012.
7. Donoghue, *On Eloquence*, p. 112.
8. Abraham Lincoln Online, www.abrahamlincolnonline.org/lincoln/speeches/everett.htm, accessed 24 November 2015.
9. Quoted in Carmine Gallo, *Talk Like TED: The 9 Public Speaking Secrets of the World's Top Minds*, London: St Martin's Press, 2014, p. 184.
10. Aristotle, *Rhetoric*, Book 3, Chapter 1.
11. William Dunbar, 'The Flyting of Dunbar and Kennedy', ll. 73–6.
12. Gallo, *Talk Like TED*, pp. 53, 66, 74.
13. Michel de Montaigne, 'Reflections on Cicero', in *The Complete Essays*, trans. M.A. Screech, London: Penguin, 1993, p. 282.
14. Aung Sang Suu Kyi, *Freedom from Fear*, London: Penguin, 1995, p. 183.
15. Quintilian, *Institutes of Oratory*, Book 9, Chapter 4.
16. Erasmus, *De Ratione Studii*, 1511.
17. Charles Dickens, 'Our Honourable Friend', first published in *Household Words*, 31 July 1952.
18. Blaise Pascal, 'L'éloquence continue ennuie', in *Pensées*, 1670, Fragment 355.
19. Charles Churchill, *The Ghost*, 1762, Book 2.

20. The sketch can be heard at www.youtube.com/watch?v=sWNEPypRJ7A
21. François Pellegrino, Christophe Coupé and Egidio Marsico, 'A Cross-Language Perspective on Speech Information Rate', *Language* 87(3) (2011), pp. 539–58.
22. Kenneth Grahame, *The Wind in the Willows*, 1908, Chapter 2.
23. See for example www.drweil.com/drw/u/VDR00112/The-4-7-8-Breath-Benefits-and-Demonstration.html
24. *Observer*, 13 November 2011.
25. David Crystal and Derek Davy, *Advanced Conversational English*, London: Longman, 1975.
26. Ralph Waldo Emerson, *The Conduct of Life*, 1860, Chapter 2.
27. *Spectator Life*, 26 September 2015.

Further reading

Max Atkinson, *Our Masters' Voices: The Language and Body Language of Politics*, London: Methuen, 1984.
    A revealing investigation of speaking strategies by modern politicians, based on audio and video recordings, with particular emphasis on the 'rule of three'.

Gyles Brandreth, *The Complete Public Speaker*, London: Sheldon Press, 1983.
    Still one of the best popular analyses of what's involved in public speaking, full of wit and personal reminiscence. Includes several short speech illustrations in full.

Denis Donoghue, *On Eloquence*, New Haven and London: Yale University Press, 2008.
    An enlightening interpretation of eloquence from a literary critical point of view, with the emphasis on reading for aesthetic delight.

Carmine Gallo, *Talk Like TED: The 9 Public Speaking Secrets of the World's Top Minds*, London: St Martin's Press, 2014.
    An informed analysis by a leading communications coach of the way TED presenters make a success of their presentations.

Sam Leith, *You Talkin' To Me? Rhetoric from Aristotle to Obama*, London: Profile Books, 2012.
    A revealing historical account of the way the art of argument has developed. Includes a commentary on several speeches.

Steven Pinker, *The Sense of Style: The Thinking Person's Guide to Writing in the 21st Century*, London: Allen Lane, 2014.

> An engaging exploration of what is involved in style, full of insights from psycholinguistic research. Not about eloquence as such, but several of the principles involved in the art of writing well have parallels in the art of speaking well.

Barry Tomalin and Mike Nicks, *World Business Cultures: A Handbook*, 3rd edition, London: Thorogood Publishing, 2014.

> Although focused on the business world, this account of the way cultural differences affect communication is informative for anyone wanting to think about eloquence in a global context.

Index of personalities

Index of subjects

Ilustration credits